AF798042

Culture and Creativity

Cultural Sociology series

Wayne H. Brekhus, *Culture and Cognition: Patterns in the Social Construction of Reality*
Amin Ghaziani, *Sex Cultures*
James M. Jasper, *Protest: A Cultural Introduction to Social Movements*
Paul McLean, *Culture in Networks*
Frederick F. Wherry, *The Culture of Markets*
Bin Xu, *The Culture of Democracy: A Sociological Approach to Civil Society*

Culture and Creativity

Claudio E. Benzecry and Vanina Leschziner

polity

Copyright © Claudio E. Benzecry and Vanina Leschziner 2027

The right of Claudio E. Benzecry and Vanina Leschziner to be identified as the Authors of this Work has been asserted in accordance with the UK Copyright, Designs and Patents Act 1988.

First published in 2027 by Polity Press Ltd.

Polity Press Ltd.
65 Bridge Street
Cambridge CB2 1UR, UK

Polity Press Ltd.
111 River Street
Hoboken, NJ 07030, USA

All rights reserved. Except for the quotation of short passages for the purpose of criticism and review, no part of this publication may be reproduced, stored in a retrieval system or transmitted, in any form or by any means, electronic, mechanical, photocopying, recording or otherwise, without the prior permission of the publisher.

ISBN-13: 978-1-5095-4686-2
ISBN-13: 978-1-5095-4687-9(pb)

A catalogue record for this book is available from the British Library.

Library of Congress Control Number: 2026938025

Typeset in 11 on 13pt Sabon
by Cheshire Typesetting Ltd, Cuddington, Cheshire
Printed and bound in Great Britain by Ashford Colour Ltd

The publisher has used its best endeavors to ensure that the URLs for external websites referred to in this book are correct and active at the time of going to press. However, the publisher has no responsibility for the websites and can make no guarantee that a site will remain live or that the content is or will remain appropriate.

Every effort has been made to trace all copyright holders, but if any have been overlooked the publisher will be pleased to include any necessary credits in any subsequent reprint or edition.

For further information on Polity, visit our website:
politybooks.com

Contents

Acknowledgments

We would first like to thank Jonathan Skerrett, former editor of sociology at Polity Press, for his encouragement and confidence in this project, as well as for guiding us from its earliest stages through nearly to its completion. During this time, we also benefited from the assistance of Karina Jákupsodóttir, for which we are grateful. We are similarly indebted to our new editor at Polity Press, Shannon Kneis, whose support and guidance helped bring the book to its conclusion. We also appreciate the assistance provided by Julia Davies and Gregory Miller, both during the transition between editors and through their direct engagement with our manuscript. Our thanks extend as well to Max Lee for his editorial assistance, to Evie Deavall for her work as Production Manager, and to Jane Fricker for copy-editing. Finally, we wish to acknowledge the careful reading and constructive comments of the reviewers – those who assessed the initial proposal and, in particular, the two who provided detailed and exceptionally helpful comments on the full manuscript. Their feedback strengthened the book considerably.

Any academic book is the product of a large community of scholars, and not just its authors. This is a central insight in the literature on creativity and one we elaborate throughout this volume. It is also deeply true of our own work. The ideas we develop here are, in part, the result of our individual scholarship and of the research on creativity each of us has conducted. Yet they are even more the outcome of what we have learned from the scholars who preceded us, from those who trained us as sociologists, and from the many colleagues and friends with whom we have discussed the themes explored in this book.

We have also learned a great deal from our graduate students, who have gone on to produce excellent research on creativity, and from the undergraduate students who participated in our courses on creativity and innovation. Their thoughtful questions and engaged discussions pushed us to further refine our understanding of the forces that facilitate and constrain creative work.

There are, of course, far too many individuals to name. We hope readers will recognize throughout the book the many scholars – junior and senior – whose work has inspired us and shaped our thinking about culture and creativity.

Finally, this book reflects a long-standing intellectual collaboration between the two authors – a dialogue spanning more decades than we care to count, and one that only now appears in written form. Some of the ideas developed here can be traced directly to what we learned as undergraduate students at the University of Buenos Aires, in Argentina. Indeed, we would not be the sociologists we are today without the outstanding education we received there, and we wish to acknowledge its formative role, including in our thinking about culture and creativity.

1

Creativity: Myths and Facts

Who is Our Leonardo?

Italy's main airport, Rome's Fiumicino, is not named after a patriotic figure, a leader of independence, a founding father, or a landform. Its name is Leonardo Da Vinci, celebrating Italy's legacy of artistic creativity. Since its inauguration in 1961, the airport has commemorated his genius beyond carrying his name; it has hosted works installed in reference to him. Some of these have been permanent, others temporary. Regardless, in all of them his genius is presented as a unique feat. In this "diffuse museum," his art is celebrated as much as his technological acumen. In 2021, for instance, a new immersive installation opened, allowing passengers to explore some of the aerospace machines he designed and learn about how Leonardo was also a pioneer of 3D-like techniques. These immersive spaces also allowed passengers to feel close to *The Vitruvian Man*, the drawing depicting the perfect proportions of the human body as defined by mathematical and geometric ratios, which is considered central to studies of perspective and modern architecture.

In just one paragraph, we have extolled the genius of an individual who transcended time and space. We have mentioned something that seems almost impossible these days, given the increasing specialization of knowledge and symbolic production at large: that a single person could master the pictorial arts as well as the study of anatomy, architecture, and flying machines, synthesizing what is beautiful and what is true. In class, we sometimes ask whether this could also happen today and what names come to mind for contemporary Leonardo-like folk. While most students tend to say that this is not possible nowadays, when asked for such luminaries, invariably, those who are named as Leonardo's current incarnations are scientists like Stephen Hawking or tech inventors and entrepreneurs like Steve Jobs.

The magic of creativity shines through in the stories of both Jobs and Hawking. Their trajectories are filled with big eureka moments, as well as with numerous idealized examples of how the rigor of a scientist merges seamlessly with the passion of an artist. In this narrative, this synergy fuels their inventive processes, continually pushing the frontiers of their respective disciplines.

The focus on where creativity happens has remained largely within a creator's head, even if some of the earlier debates about the origin of genius have faded (such as controversies surrounding the brain size of figures like Albert Einstein). In his essay "The Brain of Einstein," published in his renowned work *Mythologies*, the theorist and philosopher Roland Barthes explored the concept of genius, depicting the scientist solely as his brain: a symbol of pure intellect, simultaneously a magician and a machine, stripped of a body, personal psychology, or social identity. Jobs echoed this imagery by cloaking himself in black; his iconic turtleneck muted his physical presence, reducing him to a speaking head. Similarly, Hawking was often portrayed, due to the effects of ALS on his body, as a disembodied intellect – a uniquely thinking brain supported by advanced technologies that compensated for the limitations of his hands, mouth, tongue, throat, and eyes.

The heads of these geniuses seem like the ultimate location for where creativity lies. But then, when we listen, for instance, to Jobs' story of success, we start noticing a few factors beyond his "brilliant mind." He worked for Atari, the video game company; he associated with Steve Wozniak, a computer guru at Hewlett-Packard; on a trip to Xerox in 1979 – for which Xerox acquired 100,000 shares of Apple – he discovered the mouse, windows, icons, and other technologies they had developed, which he later remade and commercialized as part of the personal computer, bringing technology from the laboratory to the living room. Part of Apple's success in the late 1970s also had to do with deals arranged with educational institutions, as the Apple II slowly replaced the Commodore PET as the most used computer in secondary education. The picture that emerges is one less centered on Jobs' brilliance and more on his technical experience and the capacity to associate early on with other people who were at the outer parts of the center of their industry; equally benefiting from the distance to the center and to the margins. His skills consisted not just of coming up with new ideas, but also of repackaging preexisting concepts into creation and development, as well as appropriating failed designs from multiple sources and incorporating and combining them in his products. His story is one not of solitude, but of alliances with other organizations both inside and outside the industry.

Jobs was a disruptor, but his creativity did not come just from his head. It was dependent on failed experiments (by himself and others), early encounters with fellow travelers who supported his conception of himself and served as ego mirrors for what to aspire to. It was also dependent on preexisting infrastructure and technologies, as well as the results of his geographic location (Palo Alto, California, in what later became known as Silicon Valley) close to larger companies like Xerox, IBM Research, and Hewlett-Packard; universities like Stanford; and other smaller companies trying to make it in the computing business, as well as the invention of a new kind of financing now known as venture capital. In such a place, it is easier to socialize, exchange ideas with collaborators, and find the right person or piece for what he aimed to do. The story of his biggest inventions is one saturated by smaller stories of invisible labor behind him, of careers that intersected with his and moved from and into his company from other similar ventures within the larger field of technological innovation.

Jobs' origin myth persists nonetheless, and our aim in this book is not so much to debunk it as to place it in context. How does the myth of his unique creative capability relate to the broader factors we have highlighted? And how does Jobs encapsulate much of what creativity has come to mean in both public and academic conversations? We see his story as a valuable starting point for examining the present moment – one where creativity has emerged as a cultural phenomenon in its own right, extending far beyond the arts and sciences. Today, creativity is a ubiquitous buzzword, celebrated in countless TED Talks and promoted as a tool to enhance daily life. It is frequently referenced in public, political, and corporate discourse, heralded as a critical driver in diverse fields – from governmental policies and corporate strategies to scientific breakthroughs, technical innovations, and artistic endeavors. So much so that nearly every book on creativity includes a sentence like the one you just read, almost as a disclaimer. Creativity is also celebrated in spaces similar to those where Jobs began – small innovation incubators, seeking funding, inspired by DIY technologies, low entry costs, and the dismantling of traditional gatekeeping. Here, creativity is portrayed as readily accessible, waiting to be liberated from constraints and unleashed into action.

What we want to demonstrate in this book is that it is precisely those factors that enable innovation to occur in the first place. However, we have grown accustomed to the current notion of creativity – presented as a talent that some people possess while others do not. To better understand it, we need to explore its origin story. How and when did it come to signify what we now take for granted when we hear the word *creativity*? To understand the present moment, we must first trace the genealogy of the concept of creativity.

A Brief History of Creativity

Creativity, as we understand it today, may not have existed as a named concept in earlier times, but the capacity it describes has long been recognized and celebrated. Terms like originality, innovation, and genius have been used historically to signify expressions of exceptional uniqueness, whether in the creation of artistic works or the discovery of scientific phenomena. These expressions have been admired since the early modern period and became more formally recognized with the nineteenth-century institutionalization of art and science as distinct realms of human endeavor.

The term creativity first appeared in the *Oxford English Dictionary* in the seventeenth century, where it referred to God's creation. However, it did not acquire its contemporary meaning – as a specific human capacity – until the 1950s. Scholars of the history of science, art, and technology agree that the modern usage of the term only entered common vocabulary after the Second World War. By the 1970s, the equivalence between creativity and it being a capacity at the individual level was firmly established. For example, by that decade, the word already appeared in books seven times more frequently than it had in the 1950s. This trend peaked with the digital and technological revolution of the post-2000s, culminating in the ubiquitous celebration of creativity in everyday discourse that we witness today.

Today, creativity has been so thoroughly democratized and absorbed into common language that it is difficult to discern the larger historical and structural factors that have shaped both the act of creating and society's appreciation of it. How, then, did we arrive at the creator as entrepreneurial self of today? The link between innovation and creative entrepreneurship has become so deeply ingrained that we often overlook the long history of creation and the organizational systems that supported it. In the following paragraphs, we trace how creativity existed under different names, how it was organized, and the institutional and economic arrangements that sustained it.

During early modernity, when figures like Da Vinci flourished, what we now call creativity operated within the traditional framework of craftsmanship. This system revolved around workshops and apprenticeships, where a master artisan trained novices through years of hands-on practice. The process was steeped in hierarchy, emphasizing skill development and the careful transmission of techniques. Sustaining this system were wealthy patrons – monarchs, nobility, and religious institutions – who provided financial support by commissioning works. Creativity, in this context, was bound to the mastery of craft and the ability to fulfill the expectations of patronage.

By the late nineteenth century, the dynamics of creation began to shift as the rise of the bourgeoisie as cultured elite replaced the traditional patronage of the nobility. The modern art market was born, and with it, the possibility of becoming an artist was liberated from the constraints of the church and the state. This newfound freedom was paradoxically tied to money, offering a form of relative autonomy in terms of rewards and careers. The avant-garde movements of this period broke away from established norms, challenging the constraints of collective tradition and emphasizing individual expression. This shift marked a democratization of art and creativity, enabling broader participation among artists and the proliferation of ideas beyond class boundaries. Art was no longer confined to the nobility or the church; it became a space where societal norms could be questioned and reimagined.

As the configuration discussed in the previous paragraphs extended into the 1920s and 1930s, movements like Surrealism, Futurism, and Dadaism followed the avant-garde artist format. However, the postwar period in America brought a new focus on creativity that extended far beyond the arts. Creativity became a subject of fascination in science, technology, consumer goods, and advertising. The rise of terms such as "creative ability," "the creative personality," and "the creative process" reflected a growing effort to harness traits associated with artists – nonconformity, passion, moral sensibility, and novelty – for industrial and technological innovation. The cultural obsession with creativity in this era was less about art for art's sake and more about driving progress and productivity, blending artistic ideals with scientific and commercial ambitions.

In more recent history, particularly in the United States, creativity has become increasingly institutionalized through formal education and credentialing systems. The establishment of Master of Fine Arts (MFA) programs and other organizational structures introduced a bureaucratic dimension to the creative process. These institutions provided economic stability and platforms for artists, but they also imposed restrictions, creating a system governed by gatekeepers such as professors, agents, and critics. Success in these systems often depended as much on networking and credentials as on talent, with recognition being mediated through degrees and institutional affiliations that authorized individuals to call themselves creators.

The narrative surrounding creativity emphasizes autonomy, today more than ever before, largely thanks to the rise of digital technologies that promise to dismantle traditional barriers. Advocates of the "entrepreneurial self" argue that creators now have greater independence, and are able to leverage digital platforms to showcase their work, bypass gatekeepers, and connect directly with audiences. This new paradigm demands that artists also become entrepreneurs: branding themselves, building networks, and mastering self-promotion. The entrepreneurial self exemplifies a culture of creative independence, where success is framed as the result of personal initiative and resourcefulness.

This journey – from the structured hierarchies of craftsmanship to the celebrated individualism of the entrepreneurial creator – reveals that what we now call creativity has always been shaped by broader social, economic, and institutional forces. Its democratization has not erased these structures but has transformed them, creating new opportunities and challenges for those who seek to innovate and inspire.

When we shift our focus to the more recent past and delve into the actual history of when and how "creativity" came into prominence, a more grounded and complex picture emerges. Contrary to the narrative of boundless freedom and limitless potential often celebrated today, we encounter two distinct and interconnected realities. First, there is the deeply intertwined relationship between large bureaucratic systems and the modern concept of creativity. Creativity, as we now understand it, has become a category of distinction – one that is identified, highlighted, and celebrated within structures that might seem, at first glance, antithetical to it. Bureaucracies – funding agencies, expert panels, academies, certified instances for training, all often perceived as rigid and uninspired – have played a critical role in framing creativity as something unique and exceptional, worthy of recognition and elevation within societal and institutional frameworks. Second, we witness a significant shift in how creativity is understood and attributed. Historically, creativity was associated with the notion of individual genius – a rare and extraordinary talent possessed by a select few. However, over time, this idea has evolved into a broader, more inclusive understanding of creativity as a capacity potentially existing in large segments of the population. It is now seen as something that can be discovered, nurtured, and mobilized across a diverse range of subjects, contexts, and professions. This shift extends creativity into domains where it was not traditionally part of the vocabulary, transforming roles and industries that were once seen as routine or unremarkable into spaces of innovation and creative potential.

These two realities – creativity's entanglement with bureaucracy, and its movement from an exclusive to a shared capability – challenge the simplified vision of unbounded freedom. They underscore how creativity, far from existing in a vacuum, is shaped and redefined by the systems and contexts in which it operates.

So how did modern creativity stem from the bureaucratization of science, education, and consumption during the Cold War? Scholars point to different incarnations of this paradox. For instance, historian of science Steven Shapin (2020a), looking at the history of confrontation with the USSR by US scientists, shows how much the spatial program and nuclear capabilities in competition with Soviet technology drove psychologists to evaluate whether scientists had a special quality to be creative. They wanted to see if they were capable of initiative, of improvising, and whether they had the ability to imagine new forms. Could this capacity be isolated, determined, measured in mental traits? To quote Shapin (2020a: 6): "Definitions of creativity were offered; tests were devised; testing practices were institutionalized in the processes of educating, recruiting, selecting, promoting and rewarding. Creativity increasingly became the specific psychological capacity that creativity tests tested."

Relatedly, when Samuel Franklin (2023) began researching the origins of creativity's explosion in the US, he initially expected to trace its roots to the youthful counterculture of the 1960s, defined by self-expression, experimentation, and rebellion. However, what he discovered instead was that the creativity movement emerged a decade earlier – a time often associated with conformity, bureaucracy, and suburban life. The focus on creativity during this period was less about art itself and more about fostering innovation in science, technology, consumer products, and advertising. These industries gave a big impetus to a cadre of experts that started doing research on people – either to improve hiring practices or consumption – looking for their fit with concepts like "creative ability," "the creative personality," and "the creative process." Creativity became both a mental faculty and a personal attribute.

Another example of this paradoxical pairing between bureaucracy and creativity comes from historian of science and technology Fred Turner (2006), who studied the continuities between postwar scientific innovation, counterculture, and cyberculture in California. His history of networked collaboration and entrepreneurial, project-based work styles (particularly in Silicon Valley) illustrates a fascinating evolution in the cultural perception of computers and computer networks. In the early 1960s, computers were widely regarded as bleak tools of the Cold War, embodying the rigid organization and mechanical conformity of the military-industrial complex. However, by the 1990s, with the rise of the Internet and the World Wide Web, computers came to symbolize a collaborative digital utopia, shaped by the communal ideals of the counterculture that had vehemently opposed Cold War bureaucracy. Turner chronicles this transformation, highlighting the role of institutions like the Rand Corporation and MIT's Radiation Laboratory in fostering interdisciplinary, creative cultures. He emphasizes the irony of this shift, noting that the Internet was originally a Department of Defense project designed to create a resilient computer network for nuclear warfare, and Stewart Brand, a counterculture leader and founder of influential organizations and publications, played a crucial role in reimagining digital technology as a medium of openness, collaboration, and utopianism, the basis for our contemporary idea of the creative self.

Extending this line of argumentation beyond the US into Western Europe, cultural sociologist Andreas Reckwitz (2017) focused on the 1970s and the democratization of creativity – how it had been made available to a population beyond artists and experts – in what he has called "an aesthetic dispositif," consisting of new, taken-for-granted ways of evaluating work and everyday life in aesthetic terms, with an emphasis on constant innovation. He sees this articulation of discourses and techniques as coming from four concomitant transformations: a transformation in the world of artistic production, with multiple avenues to engage in artistic expression; a transformation in the everyday use of objects, with consumption evaluated more in aesthetic than utilitarian terms; a related transformation in the world of psychology of the self, coming both from the needs of the advertising industry, and the search for a self that is expressive and authentic; and fourth, the media revolution, which allowed for the combined forces of individualization, and aesthetization to merge.

In all these historical accounts, we encounter the same lesson: creativity is a relatively recent term, coined to describe a capacity that existed long before but was not previously recognized by that name. At the same time, the recognition of creativity as a particular kind of capacity helped to move the emphasis away from its miraculous and individual character into a more robust, relational, and collective exploration of the contexts, processes, and dimensions that have made it possible. All accounts show how its growth has been facilitated by large bureaucratic structures and, for better or worse, creativity could no longer be thought as the exclusive domain of genius. Instead, creativity is now seen as a capacity potentially available to most individuals.

This shift reveals the foundational paradox of creativity: it is regarded as something unbelievably valuable, yet it is also believed to be accessible on a larger scale than in the past. What are the implications of this paradox? How should we define what counts as creativity? How does creativity operate across fields as diverse as science and the arts? And, perhaps most critically, how is it achieved?

How to Study Creativity and Innovation

The past two decades have witnessed an explosion of books on creativity. There are books on how disruption, creativity, and innovation are definitive characteristics of our time, addressed to a general audience (Florida, 2002; Gladwell, 2002; Sawyer, 2006); books that denounce creativity as a new engine for domination or how it has been co-opted by capitalism (Mould, 2019; Reckwitz, 2017); and others that offer textbook-like lessons about how to make innovation happen (Rogers, 2003).

Unlike a manifesto, textbook, or survey of different fields, *Culture and Creativity* is meant to set the stage for thinking about creativity. Its aim is to lay out some of the central stakes involved in understanding how creativity takes shape. The book is situated in a dialogue with classics in the sociology of culture, social studies of science and technology, materiality studies, social psychology, social cognition, organizational analysis, social network analysis, and urban geography. It also presents some of the latest advances in sociology and related disciplines to best make sense of how foundational ideas have had a long-term influence in how creativity has been studied, as well as to highlight the research lines that are currently producing a breakthrough when investigating innovation in the arts, culture, and sciences.

Along with its close cousin innovation, creativity has also become a major area of study across a wide range of academic disciplines, including sociology, psychology, anthropology, economics, organizational behavior, legal scholarship, and the cognitive sciences. But what exactly is creativity? How can we distinguish what is creative – or innovative – from what is not? Is creativity something we can explain, or even predict? If so, what kinds of factors can help make sense of observable patterns of creativity? Rather than celebrating, debunking, or denouncing the notion of creativity, this book focuses on explaining it, with the goal that both students and practitioners learn from scholarly lessons about how creativity and innovation *actually* happen. Since a term like innovation has historically done both descriptive and evaluative work, implying a favorable judgment, what we propose here is closer to a semantic therapy, in the sense that we are interested in providing further clarity about what these terms mean. For instance, what does it mean to talk about creativity when thinking of experts like chefs and how they come up with new recipes? What when talking about lay people like "drill" musicians and how they can professionalize their music careers, since their music genre became popular on YouTube, a platform that was hard to monetize? What when thinking of how and when intellectuals rise to public recognition, and later lose it? By doing this, we hope to be able to show in each case the key explanatory factors that make creativity happen.

Creativity is typically defined as a phenomenon that requires imagination and/or novel ideas and is generally associated with the creation of new products or services. Much of what we know about how creativity happens comes from social psychology (e.g., Csikszentmihalyi, 1996; Sawyer, 2006), as well as descriptive accounts from the humanities (see Gardner, 1993). Scholars in these disciplines typically underscore imagination as the key faculty for creativity, since it is what allows creators to move beyond what they already know and toward something new by transforming existing ideas (see Koestler, 1964). This is of course an important aspect of creativity, but an account that revolves around individual mental capacities is limited in the extent to which it can explain how creativity happens.

When sociologists study creativity, they – unsurprisingly – shift the attention to the social context and point to how creativity may be shaped by social norms and constraints, but also by the accidents, contingencies, and technical adjustments that frequently occur in creative endeavors. Unlike social psychologists, sociologists who study creativity typically look at the *production* of creative objects in cultural realms, rather than the act of creation itself. Indeed, this is precisely the focus of some of the major perspectives in the sociology of culture, such as the art worlds perspective, studies of fields of cultural production, and the production of culture perspective (see Becker, [1982] 2008; Bourdieu, 1993; Peterson and Anand, 2004). Beyond the sociology of culture and its core concern with cultural production, sociologists have written about creative *action* more generally, in terms of the (extra-ordinary) ability to deviate from routine practice and delineate new lines of action (see Dewey, [1922] 2002; see also Camic, 1986; Joas, 1996).

Culture and Creativity offers an overview of a wide range of social forces that both facilitate and constrain creativity, from the most elusive (such as the nature of cognition and the social life of ideas) to the most concrete (including the role of material objects in creative work, and the organizations wherein such work is undertaken). The book is structured around a set of areas that have been central in the study of creativity: culture, materiality, cognition, and organizations. These areas not only bring attention to different factors that shape creativity, but also distinct theoretical frameworks from which to understand how creativity happens. Some of these frameworks have a long sociological tradition, going back to the inception of the discipline, whereas others are more recently developed and grounded in transdisciplinary scholarship. They each constitute a distinct perspective in the social sciences, having spawned influential bodies of work. In effect, the main areas we cover have produced knowledge about creativity with little overlap between them. In reviewing them, we try to paint as thorough a picture as possible about what creativity looks like, how it happens, and what makes it flourish or fade.

Our review attends to all the stages involved in creative work; from the initial conception of a new idea to the processes whereby the idea may (or may not) be turned into a product, and the success of the product on the market. And it includes all the social factors that shape creative work, from thinking patterns and knowledge to the materials necessary to undertake the creative work, and the social, organizational, and institutional context within which the work is carried out. This book is anchored in sociology, but, given the interdisciplinary character of the study of creativity, it also incorporates contributions from neighboring disciplines such as social psychology, cognitive psychology, materiality studies, social studies of science and technology, organizational studies, and social network analysis. We shed light on the collective character of creative endeavors, the invisible work behind some of the eureka moments we have learned to admire, how pressures to conform shape creativity, the role of material objects in creative work, and how particular social locations, and specific social and organizational arrangements inform patterns of creativity.

We focus on these four subtopics, which structure the book, as follows:

- The processes through which culture shapes creativity: the analysis of constraints, deviance, inertia, resources, conventions, interactions, institutional contexts, self-concepts, and careers, all of which frame how ideas emerge and develop. At the same time, the creation of ideas requires attention to the role of temporality in the unfolding of a new cultural object, comprising the steps through which an initial idea becomes a finalized product, as well as to the role of collaboration in generating ideas anew.
- The role of material affordances in helping (or hampering) creativity to flourish: this subtopic addresses the work of sociologists and science and technology studies scholars who have explored how objects and technologies may hinder or allow new cultural objects to come to fruition.
- The role of cognition in shaping new ways of thinking and doing: we focus on how automatic cognition can hinder *and* facilitate innovation, the role of deliberation in maintaining *and* breaking established routines, and how embodied knowledge can be a springboard for new lines of action.
- The role organizations and social networks play in the consolidation of new cultural products. This subtopic points to the embeddedness of innovation's success, so we look at organizational arrangements and social networks, as well as the role of space and place, as key factors that explain how and why new ideas become successful cultural objects.

The Organization of the Chapters

The structure of the book reflects our attempt to develop a distinctly sociological perspective to study culture and creativity. Whether studying how ideas, fashion, scientific discoveries, or artistic creation emerge, in each chapter of the book we identify and develop a series of theoretical tools to consider the dimensions, processes, and contexts through which culture shapes how creativity unfolds (or fails to). In the second chapter, we introduce key themes in the sociology of culture, emphasizing interaction, collaboration, norms, constraints, symbolic meanings, self-concepts, and career paths. This chapter outlines the foundational perspectives that frame the study of cultural production and sets the stage for exploring creativity through a sociological lens. In the third chapter, we turn to the role of objects, showing how technologies and material arrangements both enable and restrict action, and how human and non-human actors together produce culture. This chapter highlights how creativity emerges when stabilized systems are disrupted, exposing the hidden labor and innovations behind them. In the fourth chapter, we examine cognition, stressing that creativity involves more than deliberate thought or sudden inspiration, and showing how it is shaped by cognitively controlled and uncontrolled processes, embodied practices, and the surrounding environment. Foundational ideas from cognitive psychology, neuroscience, and theories of action provide a framework for understanding these dynamics. In the fifth chapter, we focus on the social organization of innovation, analyzing how social structures, fields, networks, and space shape creativity. This chapter emphasizes the importance of status, reputation, and relational ties in driving innovation across the arts, sciences, and corporate settings. Our concluding chapter has the dual mission of intervening into both sociological knowledge and the everyday lay understanding of creativity. We wrap up and integrate what we learned in each chapter about how social scientists have explored the different intersections of culture and creativity, both empirically and theoretically, and offer some ideas for how junior sociologists might study the relationship between culture and creativity in the future.

2

The Culture of Creativity

Introduction

It is close to midnight in a dimly lit club tucked away behind a nondescript storefront – the kind of place that's not quite hidden, never advertised either. The air is humid with the breath of brass and the varnish of instruments held too long in calloused hands. On stage, a quartet has just wrapped a bluesy set that dissolved into a teasing groove – one of those endings that could turn final or open into something else, depending on who steps forward. No one claps yet. There is a moment of still tension. And then, as if summoned by obligation rather than invitation, a tall man in a dark shirt makes his way up with an alto saxophone, and another follows with a trumpet. No announcements. No introductions. Just the subtle nods that ripple through the room, read differently depending on who's watching. For the musicians seated in the back of the stage, some with horns on their laps or drumsticks tapping against stools, this is not just play – it is a test.

The jam session, as sociologists Howard Becker and Robert Faulkner (2009, 2013) have shown, is less a space of unstructured spontaneity than a finely tuned system of social adjudication. Here, knowledge is not declared, it is demonstrated – and the proof is in the sound. One never says "I know the changes to this tune" – one plays them, then plays over them, then plays against them. The tune they have launched into is "Cherokee," blisteringly fast and harmonically dense, a kind of dare disguised as a standard. It is a song that separates those who merely know from those who know how to *know* in the right way. Heads nod slightly in the back. Someone mutters – grudging recognition, not quite approval: "Okay."

None of this happens in isolation. The pianist behind them – older, more seasoned – adjusts voicings on the fly, shaping the harmonic landscape in response to what's being proposed. The drummer listens more than he plays, tightening the time when it begins to slip, offering accents as commentary. This is collaboration, but it is also calibration. Everyone is listening for the moment when a musician stops merely playing and starts *saying* something – when the improvisation turns from filler to statement.

It is this intersubjective space – what Becker and Faulkner call the work of knowing in uncertain situations – that animates the jam session as a scene of interest for a book on culture and creativity. The norms are not codified, but they are enforced. Play too long, quote too much, solo out of turn, and you risk subtle sanctions: a withheld nod, or a raised eyebrow. The audience may not catch it, but the other musicians will. In this world of musicians for hire, reputations are built on the trust of other musicians, with participants excelling when they are adaptable, and know how to work with others with little preparation work. The musicians in this jazz world need skills such as knowledge of the canon, the ability to improvise when needed, to collaborate and negotiate during solos, to support when playing in the background, and to do all of this in public.

This example sensitizes us to key topics of study in the sociology of culture when thinking about creativity, including social interaction, collaboration, knowledge-exchange, norms, constraints, symbolic meanings, social psychological processes, and career trajectories. This chapter will dwell in the uneasy, generative tension between the idea of creativity as the terrain of the exceptional – where artists and cultural workers break molds, stretch categories, and disavow strictly calculative motives – and the institutions, relationships, organizations, careers, and conventions, within which they come to do so.

This tension becomes sharper when we consider the nature

of cultural markets. These markets are governed by a logic of extreme uncertainty. The value of cultural goods is not easily predictable; demand is volatile, and success cannot be deduced in advance from the inherent qualities of a work. What counts as innovative today may be dismissed tomorrow, and the same work can oscillate between obscurity and acclaim depending on shifting contexts, audiences, and evaluative criteria. This fundamental indeterminacy makes cultural markets unlike those for standardized goods.

Distinct from this general uncertainty are the mechanisms through which individuals are singled out. A small number of creators are elevated, while many others remain invisible. Here lies the paradox: collective processes of creation are retroactively condensed into the figure of the individual genius. Success becomes personalized, even though the conditions of its emergence were distributed across collaborators, networks, and shared infrastructures. Yet, at its core, creation is always collective. No matter how singular the reward may appear, or how personalized the aura surrounding an artist, cultural production depends on many hands, networks, and practices. This raises a fundamental question: how does creativity happen under these conditions?

In this chapter, we also ask: how have sociologists explained the conditions under which creativity takes shape? Should we see creativity as the outcome of the organizational and industrial settings that channel creation, distribution, and consumption, as in the "production of culture" perspective? Should we examine careers in the creative industries to identify the key elements that determine when and how creation becomes certified, and how unequal access sustains who and what counts as "creative"? What becomes visible if we treat creativity as emerging from cooperation and shared conventions, as in the "art worlds" approach? Or does it make more sense to understand creativity as tied to struggles over position, recognition, and symbolic capital, as field theory suggests? Should we instead focus on the work and ideas themselves, and the ways in which they take shape through intellectual traditions, self-concepts, and interactional dynamics?

How is Culture Produced?

In his well-known article "Why 1955?," Richard Peterson (1990) shows that in the brief span between 1954 and 1956, the emergence of rock music displaced the jazz-based aesthetic in American popular music and sparked a musical and stylistic revolution. It was not a sudden burst of individual talent, but the result of a convergence of changes in law, technology, market structure, and professional organization. The shifts opened an "opportunity space" where something new could emerge. His larger argument, elaborated later on through a series of papers and a well-known book, is that cultural innovation happens not in spite of "the system" (e.g., rock 'n' roll was imagined as a rebellion that upended all that preexisted it) but through it – when the routines and infrastructures of production are momentarily reconfigured to let in the new.

This perspective, what he calls the "production of culture" approach, proposes that we look at creativity by analyzing six interrelated fields: technology, law and regulation, industry structure, organizational context, occupational careers, and market conditions. The creativity that results is less a matter of expressive interiority and more about the capacity to navigate and rework the contours of these constraints. In this account, genres are not fixed categories but ongoing accomplishments, built and maintained through the collective labor of producers, promoters, critics, and audiences. What counts as new or meaningful is shaped by the institutional rhythms and infrastructures in which cultural producers operate.

Peterson's (1997) book *Creating Country Music: Fabricating Authenticity* offers a particularly sharp case of how this works. In it, he shows that "authentic" country music is not just about whether a singer is honest or truly from the countryside. Instead, authenticity gets built step by step by many people and institutions. Record labels and promoters put out marketing campaigns that highlight certain stories about artists (like being from a farm or growing up poor). Songs and lyrics repeat familiar themes – heartbreak, hard work, small towns – that make the music feel "real" to listeners. Radio stations, award shows, and record companies also play a role by deciding which artists and styles to support.

What counts as "real country" changes over time, but it always depends on whether the music and the image of the performer fit into a set of expectations that fans, musicians, and the industry all recognize. In other words, "authenticity" is not natural – it is something people create together, and it works when everyone involved agrees that it feels right. Across his work, Peterson invites us to consider creativity not as a rupture, but as a recombination of materials, relations, and logics – less about radical departure than about knowing how to make something feel both new and recognizable within the structures that allow culture to be produced, circulated, and consumed.

Further studies in the production of culture tackled creativity and innovation by breaking down cultural life into distinct yet connected parts: production, distribution, and consumption (Griswold, 1994). This approach moved attention away from individual creators and toward the organized patterns that shape what gets made, shared, and recognized as new. Rather than seeing innovation as flowing easily from creators to audiences, this work emphasized how each part works somewhat independently and how tensions arise as cultural objects move through them. Creativity is shaped at every step by organizations, markets, and classification systems that enable or limit what counts as novel.

Foundational studies within this perspective made this point clearly. Paul Hirsch's (1972) study of popular music described cultural industries as "processing systems" facing constant oversupply of possible products. Because demand is uncertain and production costs are low, intermediaries – record labels, radio programmers, critics, and the trade press – act as gatekeepers who reduce uncertainty by filtering and promoting a small set of offerings. These gatekeepers use established criteria to decide what counts as workable novelty. Innovation is not inherent in cultural products but the result of organizational selection processes that balance the familiar and the different to manage risk.

Relatedly, Richard Peterson and Peter Berger's (1975) analysis of popular music charts between 1940 and 1970 connected industrial structure to stylistic diversity. They showed that when few companies dominated the market, genres consolidated and styles became uniform. But when the market fragmented – often because new and independent labels entered – space opened for experimentation and new musical styles, most notably rock 'n' roll. Innovation appeared in cycles, as stable genre systems were disrupted by competitive pressures that let new actors challenge existing categories. In their later revisit, Peterson and Berger (1996) showed that distribution systems and industrial concentration shape not only how much diversity exists but also which innovations get recognized as breakthroughs rather than minor variations.

Paul DiMaggio's (1982) analysis of late nineteenth-century Boston added to these accounts by highlighting organizational form and cultural classification. He showed how nonprofit arts organizations allowed elites to reclassify symphonic music as "art" rather than popular entertainment, creating new boundaries between sacred and profane culture. Through funding and administrative control, elites secured social closure, regulating who could attend and redefining who counted as a legitimate audience. Innovation was inseparable from institutionalization and boundary-making that gave certain forms prestige while excluding others.

Other key studies built on this perspective. Diane Crane (1987) traced the art world from 1940 to 1985 to show how galleries, critics, and museums structured what counted as avant-garde "breakthroughs." Tia DeNora (1991) used Beethoven's rise in Vienna to show how patronage networks and performance venues helped define "genius" and what felt new. Beethoven took advantage of aristocratic patrons and the larger musical halls associated with them, which let him premiere his symphonies – works requiring a bigger orchestra than was common until the early nineteenth century.

Later work sharpens those levers. N. Anand and Richard Peterson (2000) traced Billboard/trade metrics in US music to show how charts themselves create genres and reward "newness" that fits the metrics; Paul Lopes (2002), writing about jazz's institutional rise, showed how museums, education, and criticism canonize innovation; Dowd et al. (2002) indicated three factors that spur the introduction of new composers into orchestral repertoires: the increased performance capabilities of symphony orchestras, the expanded resources for new music, and the proliferation of music programs among US colleges and universities.

Building on these foundations, more recent studies examine how organizational rules and evaluative systems structure innovation. Jennifer Lena (2012), in her analysis of musical genre cycles, argues that musical genres do not evolve in a linear or purely aesthetic fashion, but through recurrent organizational patterns that structure how innovation is produced, recognized, and sustained. She identifies four genre forms – avant-garde, scene-based, industry-based, and traditionalist – that map the trajectories by which new musical practices emerge, stabilize, and circulate. By showing how musicians, audiences, and institutions coordinate around these forms, Lena demonstrates that the diffusion of innovation in music is less about the intrinsic novelty of sounds and more about the organizational templates that enable novelty to travel, gain legitimacy, and be institutionalized. In a similar vein, Gabriel Rossman (2012), in *Climbing the Charts*, shows that the diffusion of new music does not follow a simple story of consumer preferences spreading from early adopters outward, but is instead structured by the institutional logics of radio programming and industry promotion. Radio airplay serves as a gatekeeping mechanism that channels attention toward a narrow set of songs, creating the appearance of organic diffusion while in fact orchestrating exposure through controlled and selective distribution. His research shows that hits spread rapidly across radio because they clearly conform to an identifiable style or genre. In this way, Rossman reframes diffusion of innovation as less about the inherent appeal of a product and more about the legibility made possible by the organizational infrastructures that determine which innovations are even visible to audiences – an argument that highlights the contingent, institutional nature of what becomes popular. Looking at the editorial industry, Clayton Childress

(2017) in *Under the Cover* extends this to the full life cycle of a novel – creation, production, and reception – showing how publishing firms, distribution networks, media, and readers' communities shape how a novel is valued and remembered. Creativity here arises from the alignment (or misalignment) of organizational practices, institutional logics, and cross-field dynamics between the creation, production, distribution, and reception circuits.

Across the five decades of cases we have discussed in this section, the punchline is consistent: what we hail as innovative depends less on creators alone than on the organizational pipelines – labels, media, metrics, formats, patrons, venues, and policies – that select, frame, and circulate "the new." Taken together, these cases advance the argument that novelty in cultural production is not inherent to the object but emerges through organizational systems of distribution and evaluation. One of their main findings is that, in cultural production, market-oriented producers have different incentives and rewards than those who orient their work to the recognition of fellow producers. Because of this, numerous scholars have elaborated on what kinds of careers exist in the cultural industries, and how much of what is creative, innovative, or considered new in cultural production is constrained by said industries. The next section answers the question of what kind of career it is to create.

What Kind of Career is Creating?

Career-focused scholarship deepens how we think about innovation, because it shifts the unit of analysis from objects (songs, books, paintings) or organizations (labels, publishers, galleries) to the trajectories of workers and the conditions under which they labor. Looking at worlds as different as those of fashion models, music industry interns, poets, magazine writers, camera people, art students, and MFA graduates shows that access to these jobs is deeply unequal. To enter and persist, workers need not just skill and creativity, but also economic resources, strong social networks, and the ability to tolerate job insecurity. Many aspirants are drawn in by the symbolic rewards of "cool jobs," but only those with the right mix of cultural and economic capital can weather precarity long enough to establish themselves. The key contribution of this line of research is highlighting how creative labor markets filter entrants: while open in appearance, they reproduce inequalities by favoring those who can absorb risk.

One of the first places this argument was advanced was by Gina Neff, Elizabeth Wissinger, and Sharon Zukin (2005). They examine how people enter and attempt to sustain careers in "cool" creative industries such as fashion, media, and tech. These fields attract workers with the promise of autonomy, cultural capital, and prestige, yet offer unstable employment with few guarantees. Because jobs are project-based, short-term, and network-driven, workers must continuously market themselves and take on the risks of such employment – what they call entrepreneurial labor. Scholarship has shown how career trajectories in creative industries emerge at the intersection of oversupply and high skill, where talented aspirants continually enter fields already saturated with capable competitors. Work is organized around short-term projects, which heightens risk while shifting the burden of investment onto individuals who must finance training, cultivate networks, and endure unemployment in hopes of securing future opportunities. The pleasures of artistic expression, recognition, and community coexist with the pain of precarity, exhaustion, and stalled careers. Para-artistic jobs – teaching, assisting, freelancing in related industries – become both survival strategies and training grounds, keeping workers tethered to the promise of artistic fulfillment. Myths of meritocracy, passion, and eventual "breakthroughs" sustain participation, fostering a process of self-selection in which workers embrace risk and self-exploitation as conditions of possibility rather than as structural constraints.

Ashley Mears' (2011) research on fashion models shows how careers built on short bursts of visibility, precarious contracts, and uneven pay affect who stays in the field and who leaves. One of her main findings is that in cultural industries, where novelty is a key element but always coupled with high uncertainty, the result is a strategy in which – for scouts, models, and clients – what is sought (the "it" of a model) emerges by discarding what might be obvious flops and following what key mediators like scouts and clients demand. Despite the systematic work of categorizing and measuring candidates to see how much they are model-like, when confronted with uncertainty, tastemakers recognize the impossibility of knowing a priori who has "it," yet keep searching for this elusive grail through incipient taste signals for success: sometimes replicating features of previous models in high demand, other times looking for those who deviate from temporary standards. Because no one can predict which style will resonate, agents and clients operate in an environment of organized uncertainty, cycling models in and out rapidly to test new looks, producing quick but unstable forms of innovation. Much of this novelty is achieved through symbolic inversions – reversing or unsettling previous conventions, as when the glamorous gives way to the androgynous, the curvy to the waif-like, or the white to the racially ambiguous – ensuring the field remains in constant motion. A second finding from Mears' book that resonates with work on creative careers shows how scouts are key in deciding who among the models end up doing commercial work (catalogues, industry shows, ads for mass-appeal companies) and which ones end up in editorial work (fashion runways, photoshoots by glamour photographers, campaigns for high-end brands). Models are faced with the choice between a career that secures less prestigious but more regular employment and the elusive chance of "making it" editorially, where work is less stable and less predictable, but comes with significant exposure and prestige (and can result, in the elusive case of "making it," in better-paying commercial jobs later).

Ailsa Craig's (2007; Craig and Dubois, 2010) research on poets serves as a key to the study of creativity as a career, showing how even in "labor of love" practices, professionalization projects are central to defining who belongs and who does not in the world of poets. Career paths depend on recognition by small presses, public readings, and grants. What looks like creative innovation in poetry, Craig argues, is made possible by institutional support that sustains fragile careers long enough for new styles to take root. Occupational closure – who gets to exclude others from participating in poetry-making – is the result of degrees that provide certification, the contacts that come with them, and professionalization projects by poets themselves, who, in opting to pursue poetry as a career (applying for fellowships, grants, residencies, and professorships), distinguish themselves from spoken-word practitioners or self-published authors. While rewards are mostly about recognition from others deemed legitimate, the structure of a poet's life is built by mimicking professional careers, even when most monetary support comes from "para" artistic work – such as copyediting, teaching writing courses for extension programs at universities, or simply working in a service job in a "creative" neighborhood. The result is the disqualification of those perceived as "amateurs" from entering the world of poetry-making. Craig's findings are similar to those for MFA graduates at large. Clayton Childress and Alison Gerber (2015) show how, for aspiring writers, a master's program serves as a symbolic resource for artistic identity; for already working writers, a source of income and community; and for editors and publishers, a signal of marketing and publicity potential.

Alex Frenette (2013, 2019, 2026), writing about internships in music and media, highlights how unpaid or low-paid entry points structure who can afford to pursue creative careers. His work shows that inequality in access to career ladders shapes which voices and ideas make it into circulation, and therefore what gets labeled as "new." One of his most interesting findings for understanding how careers affect creativity is that the ambiguity in the intern role – trapped between an educational experience, provisional labor, and the promise of a career – shapes how creative work is experienced. The uncertainty surrounding tasks, recognition, and progression can impact how interns approach innovation within their roles. He also underscores the structural barriers to innovation: internships often fail to guarantee progression to paid or creative roles, especially for those without financial cushions. Thus, the path to actual creative innovation remains structurally constrained, accessible primarily to those who can afford uncertainty and unpaid labor. Lastly, by highlighting the role of symbolic rewards ("coolness," "working at a candy store") and how being part – even peripherally – of a creative ecosystem can offer a sense of belonging, he shows how self-exploitation is sustained from the outset.

The work of Pierre-Michel Menger (1999, 2001, 2014, 2018) provides the broadest theoretical arc about how studying career paths is central to understanding how creativity can happen. In his analyses of musicians, artists, and creative labor markets, he emphasizes careers as sequences of projects unfolding under uncertainty. Innovation, in this view, is fostered not by stable employment but by flexible, project-based systems that allow experimentation – though at the cost of precariousness and inequality. His work shows that careers in the creative industries unfold within a paradoxical space shaped by the dual nature of cultural markets: the constant tension between love for the craft and the pursuit of economic interest. Like other jobs, artistic and cultural work requires discipline, training, and an orientation toward labor markets; yet it is also unlike other occupations because it is organized around vocation, promises of self-realization, and the pursuit of meaning beyond economic utility. Work in these fields is characterized by its non-routine and uncertain nature – artists rarely repeat the same task predictably and instead must continually reinvent themselves in response to shifting aesthetic norms and market demands. This generates a strong non-instrumental dimension to what is done: individuals commit themselves not only to earning a living but also to realizing an ideal of creativity, originality, or authenticity. At the same time, Menger emphasizes how difficult it is to quantify and rank talent, since evaluation depends on unstable, collective judgments rather than standardized metrics. Careers thus emerge from a constant negotiation between uncertainty, risk, and the hope of recognition, with the very indeterminacy of talent creating both opportunities for distinction and conditions for precarity.

Helen Blair (2001) illustrates Menger's theoretical insights about project-based work, career precarity, and reputation-based evaluation. In her study of British film companies, she shows how creative professionals must continually secure new contracts, with their previous performance serving as the primary signal of competence.

Because film production relies heavily on team-based work and fast turnover, reputational maintenance becomes central: every "job" counts, and the latest one often determines future opportunities. For example, Ezra Zuckerman and colleagues' (Zuckerman et al., 2003) research in the feature-film labor market suggests that actors who become typecast in specific roles may initially gain more work due to developing a clear identity for employers, but this focused identity can later restrict their opportunities for diverse roles, thereby affecting their long-term career trajectory and reputation within the industry. The key takeaway is that in creative labor markets – especially those organized around short-term and collaborative projects – workers are bound by a "recency imperative." As we have discussed, in cultural and creative industries, careers are shaped by extreme uncertainty: employers cannot easily predict future performance, and creative quality is hard to measure in advance. As a result, past achievements – especially the most recent ones – serve as the main signal of a worker's ability. Success is cumulative (a good job leads to more opportunities), while failure quickly erodes prospects. This pressures individuals to stay active, networked, and demonstrably competent, but it also makes careers fragile and contingent. Innovation in such settings is therefore closely tied to maintaining momentum.

For these scholars (see also Hesmondhalgh and Baker, 2009), people flock to creative work because it promises freedom and fulfillment that conventional jobs rarely allow: high income with flexible hours, escape from the monotony of being a "worker bee," and the chance to treat one's career as self-investment rather than simple employment. The appeal lies in the idea that work can be both pleasurable and painful, combining autonomy with risk, offering self-realization alongside the specter of failure. Structurally, creative industries sustain this attraction by keeping alive the dream of the "big job" or breakthrough that might catapult someone from obscurity to success; this search ensures individuals circulate through the field, accepting insecurity as the price of recognition.

Yet these desires are inseparable from broader economic transformations: where once security came through seniority and stable employment, careers now hinge on investment, client satisfaction, and the ability to show immediate value. Project-based work and part-time arrangements become permanent, while responsibility for conditions shifts onto the worker herself. The constant demand to "upgrade" and "update" makes self-improvement a professional obligation, reinforcing the idea that employability rests on reinvention. At the same time, creative labor markets draw on an abundant "reserve army" of aspirants willing to endure uncertainty in exchange for self-expression and recognition. The result is a paradoxical labor regime where pleasure and exploitation, freedom and precarity, vocation and calculation, are deeply entangled, each side feeding and legitimating the other.

By focusing on careers, the scholars in this section advance the study of innovation by showing how it is shaped by labor market structures: who gets sustained opportunities to create, how reputations are built and circulated, and how cycles of entry, exit, and recognition generate the appearance of novelty. Innovation is inseparable from the career trajectories that sustain, filter, and sometimes exhaust creative workers. Because work is project-based and reputations fragile, creative workers live with insecurity but also with opportunities to reinvent themselves. This allows us to explore how aspirations, risks, and structural inequalities play out. But these careers do not take place in a vacuum; rather, they happen in art worlds, made of networks of cooperation, conventions, and distributed labor. We will dedicate the next section to discussing how the study of cooperation within art worlds allows us to better answer some key questions about how and when creativity takes place.

How does Collaboration Foster Creativity?

The 1982 publication of *Art Worlds* by Becker was a watershed in the study of creativity. In the book, he proposed a unique way of seeing what art was and how it came to happen; he defined art as collective work, and as a particular kind of collective work at that, one based on collaboration. Art, he reminds us, is labor – it is a social activity. Instead of merely decoding symbolism or formal composition, or trying to grasp the artist's intention, Becker's question is both simpler and more demanding: *"How could this work have been made?"* From there, he unfolds a way of seeing that turns our gaze not only to what is in front of us, but to everything that had to happen for the artwork to come into being.

His perspective breaks down into smaller, more concrete questions: What materials were used? Where were they sourced? What conventions did the artists uphold or break? What kinds of institutional support did artists have? How did repeated routines turn into standards or conventions over time? How was labor divided? In Becker's hands, these questions are not technical footnotes, but the core of the inquiry. They are the map of dependencies, of constraints and openings, that shape what counts as art and who gets to make it. They remind us that every object we call "art" rests on a scaffolding of coordinated action, of actors, tools, judgments, and histories, woven together in ways that are anything but solitary.

Perhaps the best exemplar from this perspective is Faulkner's (1983) study of Hollywood musicians. His ethnography of Hollywood studio musicians goes beyond looking at the backstage of cultural production, inverting where we typically search for creativity. In a world saturated with mythologies of the lone genius, his musicians occupy a paradoxical space: invisible yet indispensable, technically flawless yet rarely celebrated, expressive while rarely considered authors. What we see in his careful description is a social choreography where creativity is neither spontaneous nor autonomous – it is patterned, relational, and embedded in the exigencies of professional life.

These musicians work within an infrastructure of constraints: the ticking clock of studio time, the non-negotiable demands of producers, the vague instructions that oscillate between "make it sound like something" and "make it sound like nothing else." What emerges is a creativity made of adaptation instead of escape. What makes them exceptional is less the power to innovate at will, and more the cultivated capacity to adjust, to listen – socially and musically – and to produce, again and again, something that works. Paradoxically, they create not through freedom, but through constraint; rebellion matters less than the exacting repetition of performances that must seem, each time, new enough.

In this world, musical fluency is a kind of cultural multilingualism. Musicians must move between genres, affective registers, and temporalities. They must decode partial cues, make sense of silences, and intuit what is wanted without it ever being clearly said. This, perhaps, is the central sociological insight: creativity here is not located in the object, or even the individual, but in the relationship – between the player and the page, between the studio and the set, between what is asked and what is played. What is produced here is not originality but fit. Not rupture, but coherence.

What really matters is not flashy moments of brilliance, but whether musicians and producers consistently deliver what is needed. Trust – the real currency in the industry – comes from this steady reliability. Reputations are built from the accumulation of those moments of trust. To be "creative" here is to be someone others can rely on to make music together under pressure. Improvisation is not the romantic solo but the capacity to manage ambiguity collectively, to stabilize expectations, to move forward even when no one quite knows what is going on.

This example allows us to explore how the art worlds perspective insists that no artistic product emerges from a single hand; the key is that collaboration is simultaneously broad and uneven. On the one hand, art making involves an array of participants – some formally situated within organizations and markets, others contributing from outside of them – whose skills, efforts, and resources converge in the production of a work. On the other hand, their contributions are not valued equally. The rolling credits of a film serve as a neat illustration: while they testify to the sheer range of collective inputs, they also order contributors into a hierarchy, from production companies to stars under contractual "top billing," and finally to a cascade of technical and creative specialists. What looks like a simple list is, in fact, a codified signal of status and authority, revealing how collaboration is at once horizontal in practice but also structured by power relations that decide whose labor counts as central, and whose is relegated to the background.

The division of labor sharpens this paradox. Becker asks us to consider who gets to sign a work, who is recognized as author, and who is cast as support personnel. The jazz band, the symphony orchestra, and the opera house exemplify these distinctions: conductors, directors, and soloists enjoy visibility and signature authority (Atkinson, 2006; Benzecry, 2006) while the less conspicuous players – instrumentalists, stagehands, technical staff – are named as support personnel, their efforts indispensable yet unacknowledged. In principle, roles may overlap, with the same person doing multiple things; in practice, conventions and contracts fix boundaries between high-prestige and low-prestige tasks. The rolling credits metaphor condenses this logic. Recognition is distributed, but unequally, and the form it takes – who is named first, who is buried deep in the list – renders visible the otherwise invisible structure that sustains creativity.

Combining the art world and creative careers perspectives, Menger (2014, 2018) revealed the tension at the heart of this framework: between collaboration and hierarchy within an art world. Using the idea of talent as a multiplier of the work of others in the collaboration, he inquires about who should receive more rewards because of their contributions, and what principles should govern the evaluation of collaborators – asking who is impossible to replace on a team, or what would happen if someone fails at their task (or, conversely, what happens if they do it correctly). Taking a cue from the fact that creative industries are not only uncertain but also organized as "winner-takes-all" markets, Menger shows how one tenth of creators receive half of the annually distributed income, while the top twenty percent account for eighty percent of it. But instead of focusing solely on categories like class, gender, or race, he looks at the processes through which advantages become accrued. Much like Robert Merton (1968) did in the sciences, he shows the cumulative advantages built into creative careers, and how early successes tend to generate further recognition. Examining how talent is mobilized in each role within a creative endeavor, Menger (2014) reminds us that creative careers are stratified not only by income and recognition but also by role: the "superstar," whose talent generates multiplicative effects and outsized rewards; the "guardian," whose presence is most visible when they fail to fulfill their function, since their task is precisely to preserve standards and regulate quality; and the "foot soldier," whose everyday, menial contributions accumulate into the aggregate labor that makes collective production possible. This tripartite distinction highlights how creativity is always situated within differentiated positions that sustain both the symbolic hierarchy and the practical organization of cultural production.

Recently, scholars have started to focus on a different source of variation in creative collaboration: the role of unexpected actors outside of these worlds – such as state censors – and how they reshape the terrain of creativity. Censors do not merely block or repress; they participate in the making of art by delimiting tropes, images, and references, and in so doing provide the contours against which recognition and legitimacy are granted. Alvaro Santana-Acuña's (2020) *Ascent to Glory* shows how Gabriel García Márquez's literary approach helped him to bypass the specific political critiques that Spanish censors sought to suppress during the Franco dictatorship. García Márquez's blend of fantastical elements with reality allowed him to represent political violence and tragedy without explicit political commentary. According to Santana-Acuña, in *A Hundred Years of Solitude*, García Márquez used allegory and the generational saga of the Buendía family to reflect broader themes of isolation, power, and historical violence. This distance from specific political situations made his work harder for censors to target, while still being read as a powerful critique of authoritarianism. Likewise, Jun Fang's (2025) recent work demonstrates how, in contemporary China, state censors work hand-in-hand with US film production companies, not only cutting politically sensitive material but shaping scripts from the start to anticipate both domestic guidelines and international box office demands. Here, too, censorship functions as more than prohibition: it becomes a productive force that orients what gets imagined, what circulates, and what gains legitimacy.

For the art worlds perspective, conventions are another dimension that is central to understanding how creativity unfolds. Far from being simply rigid rules, conventions function as shared norms that allow collective work to happen. They make artistic production easier, cheaper, and more predictable: everyone involved knows the "grammar" of action, the tools, and the expectations. Conventions reduce the uncertainty of collaboration, establish a common language, and provide moral legitimacy to certain ways of doing things. They are the infrastructure of collective creativity, the invisible agreements that make cooperation possible across a wide range of participants, from support personnel to star creators. Without conventions, coordination would be prohibitively costly; with them, the work of art becomes doable.

Yet conventions also constrain. They establish limits on what can be done, which materials are legitimate, and how audiences will recognize and value a work. Constraints are practice-specific: they can appear in the form of technical infrastructures, available tools (on this, see Erin O'Connor's [2025] study of glassblowing skill acquisition), or the interpretive frameworks that shape how audiences make sense of and assign value to cultural works. Conventions delimit the horizon of possibility but simultaneously give artists something to resist, stretch, or redefine. In this sense, innovation is never created ex nihilo: it emerges in relation to the already known, whether through subtle variations (such as repeating vibrato in new ways) or bold ruptures. Musical notation, for example, makes large-scale collaboration possible: a composer can write a score that dozens of musicians, who may never have met before, can all read and perform together. Without that shared system, orchestral music would be unworkable. At the same time, the very same convention constrains what counts as legitimate music. Sounds or techniques that cannot be easily captured – microtones, irregular rhythms, new timbral effects – are harder to transmit and therefore less likely to be taken up in the classical tradition. Innovation, then, often comes from pushing against or revising conventions – say, when avant-garde composers invent new notation systems, or when jazz musicians stretch classical harmony and rhythm into improvisation. Thus, conventions are not the opposite of creativity but its condition of possibility: they provide the material and symbolic resources that artists work with, while also forming the boundaries against which originality is defined.

Artistic change, within these theoretical coordinates, takes shape as the sedimented outcome of processes that unfold both within and beyond the art world. Internally, conventions provide the very scaffolding on which newness is built, since artists, critics, and audiences orient themselves around shared standards of skill, genre, and evaluation. Academic or formalist traditions turn mastery itself into a subject of art, producing works whose value lies in their fidelity to, or subtle deviations from, technical canons, while commercial settings reward accessibility and the ability to connect to broader publics, leading to divergent systems of worth. These different logics foster segmentation and differentiation, as actors create boundaries around what counts as legitimate practice, distinguishing insiders from outsiders, high art from low, or avant-garde from mainstream. Externally, however, these boundaries are never fixed: they are shaped by organizations, institutions, and audiences that provide or withdraw recognition, by technologies that alter what can be made, and by markets that valorize some forms of novelty while devaluing others. Change emerges at the intersection of these pressures, in the moments when routinization turns yesterday's innovation into today's cliché, forcing artists to push further, to shift the line of what counts as acceptable or interesting.

Innovation as a Field-Dependent Practice

To say that innovation is about the new is to miss how the new becomes recognized as such. If we follow Pierre Bourdieu (1993), innovation is never simply a matter of individual creativity or the production of novelty in the abstract – it is a field-dependent act, situated within systems of recognition and consecration. In other words, innovation happens not just because someone had a good idea, but because their idea can become legible and valuable within the field they are in. In this way, Bourdieu's theory of cultural capital is indispensable to understanding the sociology of innovation – even if he himself never framed it as a theory of innovation per se.

Let us begin with the notion of the field. For Bourdieu, a field is a relatively autonomous social space – say, contemporary art, particle physics, haute cuisine, even sociology – with its own stakes, logics, and distributions of resources. Bourdieu defines capital as the various forms of resources that individuals can accumulate and deploy to gain advantages in social fields. Within these fields, actors struggle over legitimacy, status, and meaning. What is essential is that every field has a doxa – an implicit idea of what counts as good, serious, or revolutionary work – and this doxa is not neutral. Rather, it reflects the distribution of resources within that field, which Bourdieu called economic, social, cultural, and symbolic capital.

When we say someone is "innovative," what we are really seeing is a double movement: on the one hand, the production of a deviation from the norm; on the other, the recognition of that deviation as meaningful. That recognition depends on cultural capital – not just the content of an idea, but its packaging, timing, and the credentials of the one who proposes it. In *Homo Academicus*, for instance, Bourdieu (1988) gives us a glimpse of how certain academic ideas gain traction not merely because of their empirical validity, but because of where their authors are situated within the academic field: their institutional affiliations, their intellectual lineage, and their capacity to mobilize networks of symbolic power. A young sociologist who proposes a radical new method will not be seen as innovative unless she speaks the right language, cites the right theorists, and occupies a position close enough to the dominant pole of the field to be taken seriously.

Innovation often draws on legitimated knowledge, skills, and dispositions – the very things Bourdieu calls cultural capital. Briefly, Bourdieu distinguished three forms of cultural capital: objectified, institutionalized, and embodied. The first can be seen in the art we have on the walls, or books we have on our shelves; the second in our credentials (e.g., diplomas) and the last in the kinds of bodily skills through which we signal our social position and know-how. Institutionalized and embodied cultural capital, in particular, are key for innovation, as we have seen in many examples we discussed. People with higher cultural capital know how to "play the game" in a field (i.e., they have internalized the doxa, the intersubjectively shared notion of what is valued and the rules of the game), can take "consecrated risks" that are seen as visionary rather than foolish, and are better positioned to mobilize resources, secure recognition, and convert symbolic capital (i.e., reputation within a field) into influence. In short, cultural capital can position actors as credible innovators.

In this way, cultural capital is both a resource and a constraint. As any resource, it is unequally distributed, and therefore enables some actors to innovate while excluding others whose innovations cannot be read as such. Consider the case of the Impressionists, discussed by Bourdieu (1992) in *The Rules of Art*. They were not outsiders in the pure sense. They had training, networks, and familiarity with the codes of academic art – but they also had a stake in redefining the field. They produced work that initially scandalized the establishment, but they did so by (one) mobilizing alternative forms of cultural capital, such as new aesthetic values, themes to be represented, and pictorial techniques and (two) mobilizing new forms of social capital, such as social connections with the bourgeoisie (as opposed to the aristocracy), and strategic alliances with critics and dealers. Over time, what was once deviant became dominant – not just through the power of the work itself, but through a long struggle to shift the terms of consecration and the sites where consecration was achieved (something we will discuss at length in chapter five). Innovation, then, is never neutral: it is a bid to reconfigure the field, often from a position of subaltern legitimacy, but also sometimes from the highest social positions, from those who can afford to take risks given their high levels of capital, including symbolic, cultural, social, and economic.

This is what makes innovation a social fact: not the production of novelty, but the struggle over its legitimacy (i.e., its recognition as innovation). And here is where the third aspect of Bourdieu's theory becomes essential: the agonistic dimension of field dynamics. Actors do not simply try to do something new – they try to reorient the stakes of the game itself and, in doing so, they come into conflict with others whose interests lie in supporting the status quo in the field. This is what happens when a new generation enters a field: they may reject the dominant forms of cultural and symbolic capital (what counts as "serious" music, or "rigorous" science), but they do so with their own forms of recognition in mind. They are not without cultural capital – they are bearers of *heretical* cultural capital, and their innovation is a wager on its eventual legitimacy. The history of jazz, of punk, of conceptual art – all of these can be read as struggles to revalue what counts, and who gets to count as a legitimate innovator.

Innovation often emerges from contests within fields, as newcomers challenge dominant players. This is where Bourdieu's theory links to innovation most directly: innovators may try to redefine the rules of the field (e.g., Impressionists in art, punk in music); they may come from outside the dominant group but still possess alternative cultural capital, along with social capital (e.g., connections with others who share their aesthetic inclinations and goals), which together allows them to innovate and shift what is valued in the field.

Bourdieu never offered a standalone theory of innovation; what he offered was a theory of cultural production that put more emphasis on the constraints on the creation of novel works. But his conceptual apparatus – particularly the concepts of cultural capital, field, and symbolic power – offers a way to make sense of how innovation happens sociologically. It explains who gets to innovate (those with the right kinds of cultural and social capital), where in a field innovation is possible (i.e., as fields are structured by both constraint and possibility), and how novelty becomes recognized (through the conversion of cultural capital into symbolic legitimacy).

While we cover field-inspired approaches in chapter five, it is worth discussing briefly how two key themes from Bourdieu's scholarship – certification and gatekeeping – have been engines for understanding how creativity comes to be, thanks to scholarship that has examined different instances that certify what and who is creative. Consecration describes how cultural producers come to be recognized as successful through highly visible markers of prestige. In film, for example, Gino Cattani et al. (2014) show how winning an Academy Award not only signals artistic accomplishment but also transforms the careers of directors and actors by placing them in a different tier of opportunity. In literature, Childress et al. (2017) demonstrate how the Booker Prize reshapes both the sales trajectories of novels and the reputations of authors, effectively redrawing the boundary between serious literature and the broader commercial market. In both cases, the qualities of the film or novel matter, but consecration also rests on the legitimacy of the producer and the clout of sponsors, publishers, and distributors. It can also take the more everyday but still make-or-break work of instances like movie criticism (Baumann, 2007) or book reviews (Chong, 2019).

One of the most paradoxical thematizations of the consecratory power of gatekeepers is the work of Gary Alan Fine (2003, 2004) on outsider artists. Unlike the credentials accrued in MFAs, or the prizes awarded by academies and societies, Fine shows how people without formal training or institutional backing come to be recognized as "artists." The key is the framing of their work as *authentic* – unspoiled by academic rules or market cynicism. Dealers, collectors, and curators actively produce this authenticity by emphasizing narratives of purity, naïveté, and individual genius. The biography of the artist emerges as the primary lens through which value is conferred, but crucially, it is a biography defined by lack rather than by attributes. The artists in question are portrayed as self-taught, rural, Black, and often with a history of mental illness. The absence of social capital is transformed into a source of fascination, folded into narratives of romanticism, where self-expression, isolation, and authenticity are privileged, and of exoticism, where otherness becomes radical alterity. The result is a migration from the work itself to the biography of its maker, where the oeuvre becomes legible only through the prism of marginality.

How do Individuals and Groups Produce New Ideas?

Many of the main perspectives in the sociology of culture we have introduced in this chapter focused on the context within which people in creative occupations work. Some emphasize the collaboration among many different people involved in making a cultural product; others the institutional environment that constrains what products get made; and still others, people's inclinations to succeed in their occupation and improve their social positions, and the strategic actions involved in achieving such a goal.

These perspectives have undoubtedly helped us gain a much better understanding of creative work by shedding light on the varied social factors that shape creative work and help explain what kinds of products get made and which succeed. Arguably, though, the focus on social factors has often come at the expense of the content of creative products themselves. We thus learn about the norms, values, institutional scaffolding, career patterns, and struggles over recognition that shape creative work, but not so much about how people's interests and the substantive content of their work may help explain the patterns we find in people's creative work.

A few different perspectives have begun to home in on the specifics of the work that scientists or artists do as a core element for explaining creative patterns. A prominent perspective here is the "new sociology of ideas" that was formalized as a distinct perspective by Charles Camic and Neil Gross in a programmatic piece published in 2004. The two sociologists, who had been studying the work of academics for some time, gave the perspective this name because it built on well-established traditions in the study of intellectual or scientific work developed earlier in the twentieth century, but which had lost much relevance by the end of the century, especially in the US. The two most notable traditions are the sociology of knowledge (most closely associated with the work of Karl Mannheim from the 1930s) and the sociology of science (itself associated with Merton's work from the 1950s–1960s).

Now, Mannheim and Merton's approaches to answering the question of how knowledge is produced could not be more different. Mannheim (1936, 1952) maintained that all intellectual ideas (scientific, philosophical, political) are fundamentally shaped by the socio-historical context within which they are developed and, therefore, that the central goal of the sociology of knowledge was to determine that context. This is an idea that may strike us as a platitude now, but was so novel in the 1930s that it led to the new subfield of the sociology of knowledge. Merton (1957, 1968), for his part, an American sociologist at the very core of the discipline in the 1950s, narrowed down the focus to the role of the institutional organization of science as an occupation. Merton saw science like any social institution, shaped by a specific set of values, norms, and organization. Two central mechanisms, Merton maintained, are the value of originality, given its importance for scientific progress, and the allocation of rewards for the production of scientific knowledge, which are reputational rather than economic.

Camic and Gross (2004) build on these perspectives but execute a few analytical shifts. Instead of explaining the production of academic knowledge through either the broader socio-historical context or the institutional organization of science, they zoom in on the local social context in which people produce intellectual work, attending to social-psychological and interactional processes, as well as the larger institutional, cultural, and social levels of analysis (Gross, 2003: 102). Bourdieu's theoretical apparatus – and especially the assumption that intellectuals are embedded in a struggle to achieve legitimacy and authority in their areas – is a central tenet in the new sociology of ideas, even if it is foregrounded in some cases (e.g., Gross, 2008) and less so in others (e.g., McLaughlin, 2001).

The assumption that intellectuals are instrumentally driven, constantly striving to improve their social position, made the new sociology of ideas subject to criticism for (among other things) conveying a reductive view of what drives creativity and originality in intellectual work. Gross (2003, 2008) thus complemented the Bourdieusian approach with a social-psychological theory of what he called "the intellectual self-concept." This theory is founded on the premise that intellectuals have a relatively stable understanding of who they are (or want to be) as intellectuals, and that this understanding affectively motivates them and guides their work. While the intellectual self-concept is individual, it is built around existing categories of intellectuals that are already established in the community (e.g., social activist, scientist, postcolonialist). But, for Gross, the intellectual self-concept is not dissociated from the logic of fields, so that self-concepts are not only constructed from available narratives in the field, but also guide people's work to the extent that their field position facilitates it. For instance, a higher field position (and the security of tenure) enables scholars to follow self-concepts (which may have always been there) that may lead them to make riskier choices in their work. Indeed, Gross (2003, 2008) shows this in his in-depth study of renowned American philosopher Richard Rorty.

In a very different domain of creative work, Vanina Leschziner (2015) similarly combines a field theoretical approach with the understanding that people have relatively stable self-concepts that guide them in their creative and career choices. With the case study of elite chefs, she demonstrates how chefs make choices about their work (the restaurants they work at and food they make) partly based on how they see themselves as chefs and want others to see them. But Leschziner goes further in demonstrating that, just as self-concepts drive career choices and, in turn, chefs' field positions, they also change as chefs move up in their field, in a process of constant adjustment between self-concept and field position.

The economist David Galenson (2006) also takes a longitudinal view to analyze the creative work of artists, but does so in order to answer a different question, namely what life stages artists are most likely to innovate at. Finding that artists are at their most innovative at different stages of their lives, Galenson developed a unique theory that establishes an association between life-course patterns and types of innovation. Through a study of painters' work in modern times, Galenson argues that artists can be classified into two types based on their artistic goals and work practices: aesthetically motivated experimentation and conceptual execution. Experimental innovations follow relatively vague goals and proceed through extended periods of tentative trial and error. They are more gradual innovations, and therefore typically occur in an artist's later career stages. The Post-Impressionist painter Cézanne is a clear example of this type, Galenson notes. Conceptual innovations, by contrast, are typically more sudden and radical, and therefore tend to happen early in an artist's career. Here, Galenson relies on Picasso, who famously had multiple radical innovations. Contrary to the gradual innovations of tentative experimenters, conceptual innovations entail abrupt breaks with conventions, and the ability to envision these breaks, Galenson (2006: 15) maintains, declines with experience and cognitive patterns' tendency to solidify and make change harder.

Just as individuals have been found to have predictable patterns of innovation associated with life stages, so have groups. Based on an extensive comparative case study of "collaborative circles" among artists and scientists, Michael Farrell (2001) finds clear patterns of group dynamics that are associated with creative output. Collaborative circles begin as casual gatherings of peers who know each other and have common work goals. At first, gatherings are simply social, but over time, group members become more committed to each other, and come to create a shared vision that guides their work such that the group eventually takes center stage in their creative work. That common vision eventually leads group members to collaborate on a common project, Farrell finds in his research, and the unequal distribution of tasks and differential public exposure that tends to follow ultimately leads to conflict, increasing autonomy of group members, and leading to the group's dissolution. Farrell finds that collaborative circles generally have between three and five members, and typically dissolve in about a decade, as he observed among French Impressionists, and Freud and his early psychoanalytic peers in Vienna, among other case studies.

Social relationships and interactions are also singled out as key for creative work in Randall Collins' (1998, 2004) approach to the sociology of knowledge. We discuss the structural and social network aspects of Collins' theory in chapter five, so here we focus on the more social-psychological mechanisms in his theorization of interaction ritual chains. Though his approach could not be more different from Farrell's, there are significant parallels between the two. Collins' central argument revolves around the notion that, as people engage in social interactions, they experience emotional energy (EE), and as people engage in repeated interactions with others in their area of activity, they form interaction ritual chains (IRCs), which operate as ideal conduits for EE. Think about the kinds of intense interactions that writers or scholars have with colleagues (the focus of Collins' work); these can fill people with excitement (and thereby confidence) in their ideas. Collins emphasizes that IRCs are not merely instrumental for the exchange of ideas but are also key for the high levels of EE that the hard work involved in research and writing requires. IRCs generate a strong focus of attention around shared interests, and this imbues people's mental worlds with more vibrancy than the rest of their lives, a process that is also evident in Farrell's collaborative circles. Collins finds that all creative people have high levels of EE and indeed, that eminent intellectuals tend to be not only more productive than others (a pattern Merton [1968] noted much earlier on), but also "energy stars" (Collins, 2004: 192), as they are completely absorbed by their work.

Conclusion

If creativity involves understanding how new cultural forms emerge and take shape, then studying it requires close attention to the social dynamics through which it unfolds. This chapter takes up that challenge by considering how interaction, collaboration, norms, constraints, symbolic meanings, self-concepts, and career trajectories intersect with the work of cultural production. In doing so, it situates creativity in the generative tension between exceptional acts of boundary-breaking – where artists and cultural workers stretch categories, challenge conventions, and resist the instrumental – and the institutions, organizations, relationships, and careers through which those very acts become possible. This tension is particularly acute in cultural markets, where extreme uncertainty shapes outcomes and mechanisms emerge that elevate a select few while consigning many others to invisibility.

We presented the multiple perspectives through which sociological research in culture has slowly moved away from the heroic individual account of how creativity happens. What we sought to emphasize are the manifold ways in which dimensions usually presented as opposed to creativity, such as conventions, institutions, routinary menial work, or career trajectories, are actually the conditions for it to exist. Unlike the charismatic and serendipitous account of artists as geniuses who find inspiration and produce something new, this chapter has summarized the main perspectives in the sociology of culture, which emphasize that constraints and creativity go hand in hand. While these perspectives diverge in emphasis, they all focus on understanding creativity as a collective accomplishment, built from relationships. Sometimes those relationships are structured in an agonistic way, as in the idea of the field. At other times, what is highlighted is the collaborative character of creative work as interaction. In yet other accounts, the emphasis falls on the temporal dimension, as in the idea of career, or on the division of labor and the effects it produces in assigning recognition to a few within a larger creative social world.

What emerges, then, is a picture of creativity as the outcome of a heterogeneous series of elements: collaborative interactions; conventions in notation, style, or technique; the unique realities of cultural markets as unpredictable; the stratified character of the division of labor within collaborations; and the role of gatekeepers, such as critics, cultural industries intermediaries, and even state officers. Each of these strands has been illuminated by distinct lines of inquiry, few of which can account for the others, and yet together they unsettle the view of creativity as a singular, personal, and exceptional act. What the literature offers, in its very fragmentation, is a composite sensibility – a recognition that creativity does not reside in one privileged domain but is braided out of many processes. To take this seriously is to accept that explaining creativity requires a widening of the analytic toolkit, one capacious enough to hold together the diversity of factors and the uneven ways in which they give rise to the new.

This chapter did the foundational work for the book by exploring how the sociology of culture, from its inception, has understood the creative act. In the next chapter, we explore how this toolkit has been expanded, extended, and refined through an account of how materials are also key participants in creative work, providing a better understanding of how innovation takes place.

3

What do Objects do to Creativity?

Introduction

Late at night in a cramped home studio, Wendy Carlos hunched over the Moog synthesizer, its patch cords snaking across the desk like living tendrils. Each oscillator's tuning wavered, whispering and drifting – requiring only one or two measures of precision before unpredictability crept back in. As Amanda Sewell (2020: 52) recounts, Carlos would sometimes have to "bang on the casing with a hammer to get it back into tune." Sessions stretched into marathon routines – eight hours a day, five days a week, for five straight months – on top of an already full-time job. Over 1,100 hours went into recording *Switched-On Bach*, a record that popularized synthesizer music beyond its experimental origins, reaching number 10 on the US Billboard in 1968. The Moog, cumbersome and delicate, demanded not only the skills of a musician but the resolve – and improvisational intuition – of an engineer.

According to Trevor Pinch and Frank Trocco (2002), when Robert Moog first wheeled his synthesizer into recording studios in the late 1960s, musicians hesitated – unsure whether they faced an instrument, a machine, or some unruly laboratory contraption. The wooden panels looked familiar, but the knobs, patch cords, and oscillators invited gestures closer to those of an engineer than a pianist or guitarist. To produce sound required not only dexterity but also fluency in a new technical grammar – voltage control, frequency modulation, waveform shaping. What had begun as an engineer's tinkering quickly became a meeting point where two forms of expertise – musical imagination and electronic know-how – collided. Rock performers, experimental composers, and studio technicians found themselves in uncharted territory: not simply adopting a new tool, but redefining what it meant to perform, compose, and even hear music.

The Moog was never just a neutral device, nor simply a matter of "innovation." It crystallized the entanglement of materiality, expert knowledge, and technology that underpins creativity. Its patch cables forced musicians to think like circuit designers, while its sonic possibilities compelled engineers to wrestle with aesthetic questions of tone, texture, and affect. In the process, domain boundaries blurred, and the very categories of instrument, performer, and composer were reconfigured. The synthesizer's history reveals a broader sociological lesson: creativity is forged in the dense mesh of objects, technical vocabularies, and cultural practices. Pinch and Trocco's account reminds us that each new sound or performance is inseparable from the devices that make it possible, the skills that render them intelligible, and the collective reorganization of norms they set in motion.

This example introduces the key ideas and concepts developed in this chapter. The first is the contribution of non-human actors (machinery, standards, objects) to creating culture and science, visible in concepts from social studies of science and technology (STS) such as infrastructure or assemblages, emphasizing the interface between humans and materiality. The second – and related – idea concerns the affordances these objects provide, highlighting how technologies and objects enable specific uses, generate particular states of being, and produce lines of action while simultaneously foreclosing others. The third contribution – extending from the idea of support personnel in chapter two – is the role of invisible labor: the behind-the-scenes work that makes scientific and cultural creativity possible, not just as background to bring into the foreground, but as activities constitutive of how innovation emerges. The chapter brings objects to the fore to show how, by following them as actors, we can see how they anchor collaboration, and the part tools and materials play in creating art, culture, and knowledge. It also allows us to consider when and how they act as intermediaries, simply transporting meaning or force without transformation, and when they function as mediators, actively translating, modifying, or reconfiguring the associations they pass along.

This chapter also aims to introduce the conceptual tools we use to understand a key historical shift in the study of creativity: the technological transformation – or "disruption" – brought about by the digital revolution and accelerated by artificial intelligence. Claims of technology revolutionizing how we live – and the ensuing moral panics that follow – have accompanied technological transformations since antiquity. In fact, reading the testimonies of contemporaries of the train's or telegraph's inventions, who marveled at their speed and the collapse of time and space (Galison, 2003), reveals how much they resemble ours. Yet there is something undeniable about the speed and scope with which new technologies such as algorithms and large language models (LLMs) have become agents in producing cultural products and are disrupting the organization of entire established cultural industries, such as music, journalism, literature, or film. Moreover, they have upended instances of evaluation, consecration, and distribution, like those discussed in the previous chapter.

How do Scientific Discoveries Happen?

Bruno Latour and Steve Woolgar's (1979) ethnography of the Salk Institute is one of the first pieces that fully engaged in a reconstruction of how scientific discovery came to be through a perspective that emphasized the role of human–non-human interaction in the production of knowledge. The "discovery" of TRH (thyrotropin-releasing hormone) – the hormone that regulates the body's metabolism – unfolds not as a moment of revelation but as a gradual process of stabilizing a particular molecular structure through cycles of inscription and reinscription. The hormone does not exist as a given entity waiting to be found; rather, it emerges through the laboratory's apparatus of bioassays (a test that measures the effects of a substance such as a drug, hormone, or toxin using living cells, tissues, or organisms to determine the potency, concentration, or biological activity of a substance), chemical analyses, and paper trails. Scientists begin with crude extracts from hypothalamic tissue, running them through increasingly sophisticated purification procedures while generating traces on recording devices, including chromatograms, spectrographs, and amino acid sequences.

The crucial moment comes when the laboratory's inscriptions begin to align: the biological activity (measured through bioassays), the chemical structure (determined through mass spectrometry and amino acid analysis), and the synthetic reproduction (created in test tubes) all point toward the same three amino acid sequence: pyro-Glu-His-Pro-NH2. The "fact" of TRH's structure becomes established not when nature reveals its secrets, but when the laboratory's various inscription devices stop producing contradictory results. What was initially a costly statement requiring extensive justification ("we think this substance might be. . .") becomes an inexpensive fact that can be taken for granted ("TRH is pyro-Glu-His-Pro-NH2"). The discovery occurs through this transformation – from costly, contested statement to cheap, reliable resource that other scientists can build upon without having to retrace the entire construction process.

In laboratory studies – the tradition of science and technology studies that has Latour and Woolgar's *Laboratory Life* (discussed above), Karen Knorr-Cetina's (1981) *The Manufacture of Knowledge*, and Michael Lynch's (1985) *Art and Artifact in Laboratory Science* as foundational texts – the very notion of what counts as a "new finding" is displaced from the language of revelation to the situated work of making claims credible. What in scientists' own accounts appears as a discovery – an encounter with something already out there in nature – is redescribed as the contingent outcome of practices that generate traces, transform them into inscriptions, and gradually align them into stable statements. Latour and Woolgar famously show how spectrometer readings, blots, and graphs do not arrive in the world as facts; they must be translated, interpreted, and connected through a chain of transformations until they can stand as statements. In this framing, "newness" is not the sudden appearance of something hidden in nature, but the moment when a claim has been stabilized enough to circulate beyond the walls of the laboratory.

That stabilization, however, is always precarious. Knorr-Cetina (1981) emphasizes that novelty is deeply situated within the micro-world of the laboratory. What counts as a finding in one setting may be dismissed as artifact in another, depending on the experimental routines, tacit competencies, and interpretive repertoires that organize everyday practice. Lynch (1985) likewise underscores how inscriptions and artifacts are not self-explanatory but must be worked on, assembled, and situated in order to hold as knowledge. Laboratory ethnographies in this tradition reveal that what first appears as a surprising result is fragile, vulnerable to the scrutiny of skeptical peers, to the possibility of failed replication, or to the reframing of data as background noise. Only after passing through controversy and surviving challenges does a result begin to look like a finding. And even then, once accepted, its uncertain and messy genesis is rewritten in retrospect, as if the discovery had always been straightforward and inevitable.

Just as importantly, novelty emerges as relational rather than absolute. A claim becomes new in relation to the existing literature, to what competitors are producing, and to the rhetorical space available in journals and grant proposals. Novelty is produced in writing as much as in experimentation, through the crafting of arguments that locate a result against what came before and emphasize its difference. From this perspective, "new findings" do not appear as singular breakthroughs but as the outcome of extended processes: the translation of inscriptions, the negotiation of controversies, the closing down of alternative interpretations, and the careful positioning of claims within a broader field. Laboratory studies thus shift the focus from discovery as the uncovering of nature to discovery as the work of manufacture and stabilization, showing how what we call "new" emerges through the practices, alignments, and institutional supports that render statements durable, credible, and transportable. In the next section we show how the best entry point to study this are, paradoxically, the moments in which this ecology gets unsettled, allowing us to see the work it takes to render an association between practices, alignments, and institutional support stable for a long period.

What is in an Infrastructure?

Stephen Hawking was undoubtedly recognized as one of the geniuses of our time. His work on black holes, relativity, and the origins of the universe earned him a prestigious professorship at Cambridge – once held by Isaac Newton – as well as multiple awards including the Fundamental Physics Prize, the Copley Medal from the Royal Society, and the Wolf Foundation Prize, which recognizes achievements across disciplines. He became known to wider audiences through his mission to bring expert knowledge on the universe's beginnings, the existence of multiple dimensions, and time's relativity to lay readers, especially after the 1988 publication of *A Brief History of Time*. He extended this reach through television, conferences, lectures, and meetings worldwide. Despite living most of his adult life with ALS, a disease that slowly paralyzed him, Hawking became one of the most recognized public intellectuals of the twentieth century.

In *Hawking Incorporated*, Hélène Mialet (2012) examined the infrastructures that enabled such achievement given his bodily limitations. Drawing on fieldwork and interviews with colleagues, journalists, engineers, assistants, and nurses, she reconstructed the networks of humans and machines that allowed Hawking to live and work. Countering the mass media portrayal of Hawking as a genius precisely because of his non-functioning body, Mialet instead shows him as embodied through a distributed assemblage of assistants, nurses, and devices that connected him to helpers, audiences, colleagues, and journalists.

Hawking communicated through a voice synthesizer, transforming muscle twitches into text with predictive systems that completed words and sentences before sending them to a speech synthesizer. His distinctive synthetic voice – known as "Perfect Paul" – originated from MIT engineer Dennis Klatt's DECtalk system, later adapted into the Speech Plus CallText 5010 hardware. This voice became intimately tied to his identity; even when offered upgrades, he insisted on keeping the original. As the CallText hardware aged and became fragile, a team of collaborators – including graduate assistants, engineers, and Intel researchers – embarked on a project to emulate the synthesizer in software. Their aim was to preserve the voice's exact sonic character while making the system more reliable and maintainable. A dedicated team reverse-engineered the aging Speech Plus CallText 5010 hardware and built a software emulator that faithfully reproduced Hawking's iconic "Perfect Paul" voice. After extensive work, they averted the crisis surrounding Hawking and the voice that identified him.

This process offers an eye-opening entry point for understanding how and when things become unsettled, or cease to function as "black boxes," in the parlance of science scholar Latour (1987). As we saw previously, objects, facts, and our understandings become stabilized over time, allowing for normalized and routinized actions. Precisely when things are destabilized – as in the case of Hawking's voice – we get to "open" these black boxes and examine them, revealing the extensive work behind mutual understandings and the innovations that arise when established patterns are disrupted.

Mialet shows how Hawking's productivity was not the outcome of an isolated mind but of a distributed network of human and non-human actors that collectively formed an "extended body." Different agents performed distinct functions – an assistant offering memory, a machine producing voice, a collaborator sketching equations – sustaining cognition as dispersed rather than self-contained (as we discuss in more detail in chapter four). The speech synthesizer not only translated Hawking's thought into communication but also generated a recognizable style inseparable from his persona. This prosthetic voice stabilized his public presence even as the underlying technologies strained to keep pace with his evolving sense of self.

Hawking's life also reveals how such assemblage required transforming him into a binary actor whose competences emerged only through reorganizing the world around him. His participation is literally mediated through binary code – the computer interface, the speech synthesizer, the technical assemblages that allow him to communicate. Rather than being a "natural" autonomous actor, he becomes an actor who exists through this human–machine coupling. The world around him had to be reconfigured – from modified wheelchairs and voice software to teams of collaborators and publicity channels – so that Hawking could appear as the singular figure "Stephen Hawking." Assistants translated external complexity into digestible units, filtering sensory and informational input into usable forms. Repetition and pre-programming, far from being mere accommodations, became central strategies: standardized routines stabilized fragile processes, enabling continuity across unpredictable encounters. Machines did not simply transmit ideas but participated in their production, inserting themselves into the very act of writing and dissemination. From this vantage point, Hawking appears less as an isolated genius and more as the outcome of recursive relations among people, devices, and practices of repetition that collectively sustained his authority.

This example points to the organization of creativity as a particular kind of infrastructure. Drawing from Susan Leigh Star's foundational insights into infrastructure and invisible work (see Star and Ruhleder, 1996; Star and Strauss, 1999), an ecological view of creativity reveals the vast, interconnected web of taken-for-granted elements that must align for creative production to emerge. This perspective shifts our attention toward the mundane yet essential substrates that make creativity possible: the warehouses that store materials across time, the repair work that maintains tools in working order, the non-human agents – from software algorithms to material properties – that participate as active collaborators in the creative process. What appears as individual inspiration is but the visible tip of an enormous iceberg of infrastructure, where countless routine practices, storage systems, and maintenance activities create the conditions of possibility for creative work. The ecological view asks not *who is creative?* but rather *what assemblage* of human and non-human actors, institutional arrangements, and material conditions converges to enable this particular creative outcome?

Hawking was the effect of multiple technologies, prompting us to ask to what degree machines extend human capacities and, conversely, to what extent we depend on our environment as much as he did. By foregrounding these arrangements, we can better grasp what happens when we center the technologies of knowledge and art. This precise calibration allows us to see all the actors assembled in an infrastructure relationally, while also considering how each one contributes to it. In the next section, we begin unraveling how humans and non-humans participate in producing knowledge and culture and when and how they generate innovation.

What do Objects Let Us do?

Understanding the materiality of culture begins by taking stock of the affordances that objects allow for – and those that they preclude. How resistant are materials to what we would like them to do? What lines of action do they allow for? What do they nudge us toward? Sociologists, psychologists, design scholars, and researchers from the STS tradition have given us a series of concepts (*affordances*, *unruly/docile objects*, *boundary objects*) to make sense of these questions in the worlds of creativity, cultural production, and science.

The concept of affordance (Gibson, 1979) highlights how technologies and objects enable specific uses, generate particular states of being, and produce lines of action, while simultaneously foreclosing others. In design, affordances refer to the aspect of an object that shapes its functions and operations (Norman, 1988). They operate through interrelated mechanisms by which objects request, demand, allow, encourage or discourage, and refuse (Davis and Chouinard, 2016). One of the most pertinent uses of this concept for this book is DeNora's (1997, 2002) account of Beethoven's innovations, showing these were not only compositional but also deeply shaped by material, technological, and social conditions. In DeNora's framing, affordances are the action possibilities an environment, object, or instrument makes available to an agent; they are relational, not inherent. This perspective lets us see Beethoven's creativity as emerging in dialogue with the pianoforte, the concert hall, and the evolving orchestra, rather than purely from internal genius producing abstract ideas. The pianoforte's affordances – its wider dynamic range, capacity for nuanced expression, and ability to sustain long phrases – enabled Beethoven to experiment with textures, dynamics, and dramatic contrasts impossible on earlier harpsichords. Its material properties effectively "invited" certain gestures: sudden sforzandos, powerful crescendos, and expansive melodic lines. In this sense, the piano was an active participant in shaping composition. Likewise, larger halls and more standardized orchestras allowed Beethoven to conceive symphonic and piano concert works projected over greater distances with more nuanced color. The spatial and acoustic properties of these venues, along with the growing professionalism of orchestras, made possible the dramatic, virtuosic gestures that characterize his later works. In short, the environment and instruments were not passive backgrounds but co-actors scaffolding the innovations we now associate with Beethoven.

Music has been a fruitful milieu for exploring the role technologies play in fostering innovation. Antoine Hennion (1999) shows how the revival of Baroque music in the late twentieth century would be impossible to understand without examining technological mediators – recording technology, sound reproduction systems, and other devices – that do not simply transmit Baroque music but reshape how we experience and love this music today. Rather than delivering "authentic" Baroque music, these technologies actively create our contemporary relationship with it. Hennion demonstrates how modern recordings gave musicians a new standard for performing Baroque music, rather than following the inherited symphonic style of the nineteenth and early twentieth centuries. This is the paradox of the Baroque revival: the capturing of music on record enabled its freedom. Recording was powerful enough to give life to a historically informed style of play, deemed more authentic – using or recreating Baroque instruments such as gut strings, wooden flutes, natural horns without valves, smaller orchestras, and harpsichords instead of pianos, all producing fundamentally different timbres and dynamic capabilities. Yet the innovation in this revival was in fact a return to earlier forms, a departure from how contemporary performers had approached the style until the historicist school of Baroque performance emerged, one more akin to the large symphonies of Mozart, with modern instruments and Romantic-era interpretive conventions such as steel strings and oversized orchestras.

In *The Pasteurization of France* (1988), Latour gave us another conceptual tool to make sense of what objects let us do: he coined the dichotomy of docile and unruly objects to show that microbes, laboratories, and hygienic technologies were not simply passive carriers of Pasteur's genius, but actants that had to be enrolled and disciplined into networks. In Latour's account of the acceptance and adoption of Pasteur's findings about microbes, infections, and how to prevent them, docile objects (like the microbe) are those that have been successfully enrolled into networks and stabilized. They act as "obedient allies," carrying Pasteur's claims across domains (from lab bench to hospital ward to dairy farm) without too much resistance. They "behave" because their functions, affordances, and roles are predictable. These objects appear mundane precisely because they fulfill their delegated tasks silently. Unruly objects, by contrast, are those that refuse stability. They leak, break down, resist, or act in ways that exceed the roles assigned to them. They reveal the hidden labor of maintenance and the fragility of socio-technical arrangements. For Latour, such breakdowns or refusals are analytically precious: when an object becomes unruly, it exposes the networks of humans and non-humans that must be mobilized to repair, adjust, or redesign it.

The case of the contemporary art museum is an inviting entry point to see the relationship between the docility (or not) of objects – not in the sciences, where this phenomenon was originally studied, but in the arts; in his study of the Museum of Modern Art (MoMa), *Still Life*, Fernando Domínguez Rubio (2020) compels us to see artworks as unstable, materially unruly objects whose very existence as "art" is precarious and negotiated. In contrast to traditional aesthetic frameworks that center on authorship and originality, Domínguez Rubio invites us to examine how artistic objects become stabilized – and thus recognizable – through institutional routines that are anything but neutral. Contemporary works like performances, digital installations, or organic assemblages disrupt the assumptions that sustain museum practice: that works can be preserved, transported, and shown without altering their identity. Their resistance to standard conservation protocols redefines what creativity entails. No longer confined to the moment of artistic creation, creativity becomes a distributed, infrastructural effort – one shaped by curators, conservators, technicians, and the very objects that refuse to behave. Artistic innovation here lies not only in inventing new forms but in grappling with how those forms challenge the regimes of visibility, durability, and legibility that define the museum's authority.

This reframing reveals how institutions tasked with preserving culture are also spaces where creativity is continuously transformed under pressure. In this account, the museum operates as an "objectification machine," as Fernando Domínguez Rubio and Elizabeth Silva (2014) put it, one that seeks to render volatile things legible by stripping them of their variability. Yet the labor of stabilization – what Domínguez Rubio calls *mimeographic* work – is never complete, particularly when confronted with objects that resist standardization. Here, aesthetic value is not simply interpreted but actively constructed through material choices, dilemmas about what the work of art is, and contested judgments about what makes a work the "same." The dilemmas are concrete: if a video installation is tied to obsolete playback equipment, is it still the same work if migrated to a digital format? If an installation includes organic materials that decay, should they be replaced to simulate permanence, or left to disintegrate as a condition of its ontology? His account of museum work and disruption shows how unruly works of art challenge the categories through which art has been conceived since modernity. They force us to imagine a work of art that is not unique – a digital piece, for instance, is distributed across multiple formats and files. It no longer relies on the idea of originality, since what is exhibited may be a copy or the support materials for the work itself, as in a performance. Nor can it depend on the notion of solo authorship, for digital works cannot survive, circulate, or even be exhibited without the intervention of many actors beyond the artist. It is here, in the tension between docile and unruly, that questions about the material contributions to creativity emerge most forcefully. The museum's practices are not simply about managing art but about negotiating the capacities and resistances of matter itself.

Scholars in this tradition, which sees the technical and the social as co-constitutive, have also invoked the role of materiality, more precisely what they call boundary objects (Star and Griesemer, 1989), in explaining how certain objects facilitate communication between multiple constituencies. These objects serve as points of reference, allowing the translation of the common object into multiple logics. Materials remain flexible for group use and capture forms of nonverbal knowledge; they are elastic enough to adapt to local needs and constraints, yet robust enough to maintain a common identity across sites. The most famous example is the specimen in natural history: the same bird or plant sample could be used by amateur collectors, local guides, and professional scientists, each group interpreting it differently while still recognizing it as the "same thing." Its standardized form – catalogued, labeled, and stored – allows it to travel across settings and coordinate work without requiring complete agreement on meaning (Star and Griesemer, 1989).

A further case of knowledge and innovation – focused on the politics of territorial control in seventeenth-century France through the construction of the Canal du Midi – comes from Chandra Mukerji (2009). She emphasizes how survey maps, waterworks, design drawings, and even the canal itself mediated between court politics, peasant knowledge, and engineering practice. The maps and plans were flexible enough to be used by court elites, engineers, and local peasants, yet standardized enough to coordinate action across groups. The hydraulic structures – locks or reservoirs – were objects carrying different meanings for state actors (symbols of mastery), engineers (technical solutions), and local laborers (work routines, grounded in land and water).

Through this lens, innovation appears as the ongoing coordination of multiple forms of expertise, infrastructures, and meanings that converge, often imperfectly, around shared yet contested objects. The emphasis in thinking through objects is to understand how stability is achieved and maintained, and the possibilities and difficulties materials present in making it happen. The earlier MoMA example showed the opposite of what a boundary object does: the challenge that new artistic forms (installations, performances, video art) pose to preexisting infrastructures.

These dynamics of boundary objects – how they coordinate multiple constituencies while remaining flexible enough to accommodate different meanings – extend beyond specimens and infrastructure to encompass the spaces and rituals of sociability themselves. When objects, practices, and settings converge to facilitate exchange between different worlds of expertise, they function not merely as backdrops but as active participants in innovation. In "Breakfast at Buck's," Shapin (2020b) demonstrates this principle: in Silicon Valley's breakfast culture, a seemingly ordinary restaurant becomes a carefully orchestrated assemblage where material culture, temporal liminality, and face-to-face sociability combine to produce the conditions for techno-scientific future-making.

Shapin proposes an account of how techno-scientific innovation is produced and the role that spaces of culinary sociability play in that process. In his well-known study of truth, *A Social History of Truth* (Shapin, 1994), truth emerges as a historically situated social convention, grounded in the moral economy of early modern gentlemanly culture, in which norms of honor, trust, civility, and credible testimony structured who could be believed, under what conditions, and with what authority. In his article on breakfast, sociability, and innovation, he offers a genealogical ethnography of one of the spaces in which such interactions take place: a Californian breakfast setting where techno-scientific innovation aimed at transforming niche or experimental technologies into commercially viable products for broader publics is enacted and produced. The study focuses on Buck's restaurant in Woodside, California: a seemingly ordinary breakfast spot that has become legendary in Silicon Valley folklore as the birthplace of companies like Netscape, PayPal, Hotmail, and Tesla – a place where venture capitalists and entrepreneurs have conducted billions of dollars' worth of deals over breakfast meetings at its rustic tables since the early 1990s.

Through meticulous attention to the material culture of Buck's – from its intentionally chaotic "American whacky" decor featuring enormous ketchup bottles, model airplanes, and a twenty-foot wooden fish, to its paper placemats that became the medium for sketching business plans – the article demonstrates how this space operates as a carefully constructed stage-set for future-making, where the informality of breakfast (a meal of culturally unstable identity that exists outside the normal working day), the intimacy of face-to-face interaction, the high-bandwidth monitoring possibilities of shared meals, and the restaurant's "neutral territory" status combine to create the perfect conditions for the kind of visionary, often utopian conversations that characterize Silicon Valley innovation. Shapin's analysis focuses on the role of settings, sociability, and both spoken and unspoken elements in the enactment of breakfast as a socio-technical and interactional arrangement among investors and entrepreneurs, and on how this arrangement comes to function as a quasi-object, stabilized across the perspectives of the different actors involved.

When are Objects Mediators? When are they Intermediaries?

This section turns to the role of technological mediation in disrupting established patterns of cultural consumption, distribution, and evaluation. Such research gains new salience as our lives become increasingly mediated through technologies that not only reshape cultural habits but also "make sense" of us by registering and categorizing actions, inferring future behaviors, and acting pre-emptively upon them.

Over the past four decades, the cultural landscape of music – and by extension, cultural production more broadly – has been fundamentally disrupted. Scholarship has worked hard to describe the collapse of older cultural forms and the unstable emergence of new ones. Where music once circulated primarily as a material commodity – embodied in CDs, tapes, or LPs, each format carrying distinct listening rituals and social hierarchies – the migration to compressed digital files and now to streaming platforms has dissolved the physical and temporal boundaries that once structured listening practices (Sterne, 2012). The shift does not simply substitute one technology for another but alters the very conditions of engagement: rituals of anticipation, purchase, and repeated play have given way to a continuous stream of machine-curated content, where music appears as background, detached from the intensities of collective listening. According to Hennion (2001), music has become de-ritualized and de-classified, as distinctions of genre, taste, and expertise blur into individualized consumption patterns, replacing the always social and ritual music of the past – music that once existed only in specific contexts – reassembled endlessly in playlists that circulate across platforms and social networks.

This logic of "total availability" (Reynolds, 2011) both expands and impoverishes culture: hypertrophic production leads to atrophy of attention, and the obsessive recycling of past styles into ever-new hybrids. What emerges is a low-cost, infinite-inventory system where value shifts toward platforms rather than artists. In this sense, culture today is not simply transformed but destabilized, its rituals hollowed out and its forms proliferating so rapidly that the very conditions of cultural experience have shifted from scarcity and reverence to abundance and indifference. The advent of "content" as the dominant term for cultural and artistic products – music, movies, television – captures perfectly the emphasis on the "hardware" of culture: its distribution and consumption. The wording is fitting, since this version of culture is always available, contained, stored, and retrieved.

While this diagnostic is shared by both experts and lay people, such sweeping accounts need to be disaggregated into smaller queries to be better understood and interrogated with more precise conceptual tools. In this section, we show cases of disruption (in music and journalism, especially) to examine how new configurations bring about new divisions of labor, new forms of authorship and authority, new career patterns, and shifting instances of consecration. For STS, these new digital technologies are not peripheral but an object to be analyzed in their materiality, and the effects they have. They do more than provide the tools through which cultural goods are produced and circulated; they actively generate new patterns of relationships that reconfigure how creativity takes shape. By transforming key dimensions of cultural production – such as the organization of labor, the forms of collaboration, the mechanisms of distribution, and the criteria of legitimacy – technologies become constitutive of the very processes that in chapter two appear only as technical background. Seen in this light, the impact of new technologies is not incidental but central: they alter both production and consumption, giving rise to novel modes of evaluation, standards of certification, and pathways of recognition, as well as novel modes of creation.

Cultural critic John Seabrook's (2012, 2015) essays on the transformation of music production shows how Swedish producers reshaped the global soundscape for electronic and dance music, and how they reorganized the very structure of making music into an assembly line that blurs artistry and craft, invention and formula. Producers – not singers – sit at the center, dissecting songs into modules (hook, bass line, drop, bridge), each crafted by specialists whose expertise stems less from inspiration than from technical acuity and iterative recombination. In this system, European melodic sensibilities and American rhythmic traditions are not reconciled but sutured together, yielding tracks designed for maximum consumption across markets. What emerges is a new gendered division of labor, in which young women often provide the vocal raw material – emotive yet interchangeable – while mostly male producers and engineers dictate structure, texture, and finish. Support personnel for sound mixing are supplanted by software, plug-ins, and automated mastering tools. At the same time, niches are created for figures who might once have failed as soloists but now find durable roles as topliners, track builders, or comp writers – new careers born from the dismantling of old ones, all in service of a machine that deconstructs, reassembles, and endlessly iterates what counts as a "hit."

Let us now look closely at one of the professions most affected by this disruption: recording engineers (Siciliano, 2016, 2021).

In Michael Siciliano's account, their work illustrates a broader reorganization of cultural labor in which individuals are increasingly pushed into entrepreneurial modes of self-making. Rather than secure, salaried positions in large studios with fixed hierarchies and clear divisions of labor, engineers now work project by project, piecing together irregular, often underpaid "gigs" in a competitive market where the boundaries between creative and service labor blur. They do not only engineer sound: they cultivate clients, manage publicity, maintain a presence on social media, invest in and upgrade equipment, and assume financial risks once borne by studios. Even engineers with reputations and mid-career experience report worries over precarity, unstable prospects, and fragile recognition, since names may be omitted from credits in ways that matter profoundly for professional standing. Autonomy over the day-to-day may increase, but control over how one's contributions are valued decreases. What emerges is a figure who is simultaneously technician, producer, entrepreneur, and marketer, responsible for infrastructure and client relations as much as for technical expertise. Technological innovations such as digital audio workstations, home studios, and remote mixing expand capacities and lower barriers to entry, yet they also saturate the field with competition, forcing engineers to constantly update skills while diluting the distinctions between engineer, mixer, and producer. In this way, the engineer exemplifies how disruption in the music industry has reorganized its functions, roles, authority, and systems of recognition.

At the level of new actors in the music world – streaming platforms and algorithms – Nick Seaver's (2018, 2022) study of people who make music recommender systems uses the language of traps and nudges to describe how cultural techniques, infrastructures, and recommendation systems shape action without fully determining it. The logic is not that systems force people into a single path but rather that they arrange environments so certain outcomes are more likely. A nudge works by subtly steering behavior – presenting some options more prominently, framing choices to encourage one selection over another, or embedding small frictions that push users toward specific actions. A trap, by contrast, closes off alternatives, structuring the field such that once one has stepped in, it becomes difficult to exit or do otherwise.

For Seaver, this distinction illuminates how algorithms, platforms, and cultural systems exercise power: not simply through coercion or command but by configuring the conditions under which choices are made. Their logic is one of shaping practice through design and arrangement rather than overt imposition, much like the dynamics of traps and nudges that either foreclose alternatives or subtly steer actors toward outcomes. In this sense, the question becomes whether actors – human or not – function as intermediaries, merely transmitting meaning, or as mediators, to borrow from Michel Callon (1986) and Latour (2005), distorting, transforming, and generating effects as they circulate within the system. Algorithms, in particular, emerge as new mediators of cultural life: not passive carriers of intention but agents that structure possibility, recalibrate relations, and intervene in the production of meaning, thereby enacting non-human agency at the heart of social practice.

The work of Tarleton Gillespie (2014, 2018) on platform governance and moderation exemplifies how platforms and algorithms have reconfigured the gatekeeping of taste: authority no longer resides solely in critics, editors, or cultural institutions, but is embedded in design choices that govern use, making recommendation itself a form of governance. In an algorithmic – rather than purely mechanical – sense, this involves classifying users, tracking and aggregating behavior, and predicting preferences through external "signs" and clusters of data, all optimized for engagement. What emerges is a mode of authority less about explicit evaluation and more about infrastructural design when recommending what we should watch or listen to next. The algorithm structures future options by nudging us toward cultural objects that resemble our preexisting choices and those of others who share our taste and demography.

Transformations in platform technologies have particularly affected journalism. While the relevance of algorithms is obvious, we focus instead on changes brought by digitalization that shape what gets signaled as relevant, how metrics impact editorial decisions, and how the appearance of digital-only media alters journalistic recognition. On the first, Pablo Boczkowski (2010) shows how the migration of news online changed the pace of consumption – real-time instead of morning or afternoon – and its availability. His foundational work on the digitization of news foregrounds how technological change reshapes journalism not simply through speed or access, but through new competitive dynamics that reorganize editorial judgment itself. As news migrated online, temporal rhythms shifted from periodic cycles to continuous, real-time publication, dramatically expanding availability while simultaneously intensifying inter-outlet surveillance. This ease of monitoring competitors produced what Boczkowski identifies as homogenization: journalists increasingly mimic rival coverage to avoid missing stories, narrowing the range of topics and perspectives despite an apparent explosion of content. The result is a transformation of professional practice in which editorial autonomy is subtly displaced by reactive, market-oriented logics embedded in digital infrastructures.

To understand how metrics impact editorial decisions, Caitlin Petre (2021) studied *The New York Times*, *Gawker*, and Chartbeat to explore how performance metrics transform journalism, showing how they influence morale and, in non-legacy newsrooms, shape editorial decisions. Petre's analysis of metrics in newsrooms offers a fine-grained account of how quantification reshapes journalistic labor from the inside, altering both affective orientations and organizational authority. Through her study of legacy and non-legacy outlets, she shows that metrics are not merely informational tools but moral and emotional technologies that structure evaluation, motivation, and worth. In legacy institutions like *The New York Times*, metrics circulate cautiously, shaping morale without fully displacing professional norms; in contrast, in digitally native newsrooms, metrics become central to editorial decision-making, redefining what counts as success. Petre demonstrates how data-driven visibility creates new hierarchies among journalists, privileging those who can translate audience attention into measurable performance. Her work reveals metrics as sites of struggle, where professional identity is negotiated between ideals of journalistic judgment and the demands of quantifiable popularity.

On how much journalistic recognition has been transformed, Angèle Christin (2020) documents how, when news moved online, journalists suddenly learned what audiences actually liked through algorithmic tracking of web traffic and activity, fundamentally changing their understanding of both audience and role. Christin's ethnography of algorithmic journalism captures the epistemic shock produced when journalists encountered audience behavior through the lens of real-time data. As news organizations moved online, journalists gained unprecedented insight into what readers clicked, shared, and ignored; knowledge that unsettled long-standing assumptions about audience taste and journalistic authority. Christin conceptualizes this tension through the evocative opposition of "Pulitzer or Clicks," a frame that crystallizes the conflict between traditional markers of professional excellence and the imperatives of digital visibility. Her work shows how data analytics introduce new forms of reflexivity and anxiety, transforming journalism into a field organized around continuous audience feedback and the uneasy coexistence of symbolic prestige and numerical success.

Transformations in platform technologies have particularly affected creative labor in digital media, the spaces that were supposed to brim with creativity once the chains of legacy institutions were broken. Brooke Erin Duffy's (2017) *(Not) Getting Paid to Do What You Love* examines how social media platforms reshape creative work through what she terms "aspirational labor" – enjoyable yet exploited work oriented toward future gains rather than present compensation. This concept captures how young women, especially in fashion, beauty, and lifestyle content creation, convert consumption into production, performing unpaid relational work while hoping for eventual monetization. Duffy reveals the gendered dimensions of this economy: historically feminized spaces of consumption become sites where women perform invisible, emotional labor – responding to comments, reciprocal tagging, cultivating authenticity – measured by social media metrics that serve as currency for status and achievement. The book illuminates tensions between authenticity and self-branding, where creators must maintain "calculated authenticity" while remaining constantly "on" for imagined audiences. Her framework of aspirational labor exposes the gap between romanticized narratives of creative entrepreneurship and practical realities, where visibility remains perpetually deferred, unpaid work proliferates, and commodity feminism masks persistent gender inequalities in who gets paid to do what they love.

Lastly, in a paper that shows the pervasiveness of the new norms created by influencers, Sophie Bishop (2025) shows what happens when the same processes we observed for the practice of journalism take root within the art world. She calls this "influencer creep," which operates through three interconnected tenets: self-branding, optimization, and authenticity. Her work reveals how artists increasingly appropriate self-branding techniques fundamentally rooted within influencer cultures, adopting strategies previously foreign to their professional norms. These practitioners simultaneously take up calculated techniques of algorithmic optimization; much like Duffy's fashion bloggers, they share increasingly intimate dimensions of their authentic – yet, paradoxically, highly stylized and curated – selves online, performing vulnerability as strategic capital. According to Bishop, influencer creep generates accelerated, relentless demands: artists must now consistently perform and vigilantly maintain coherent artistic identities across multiple, often contradictory social media platforms simultaneously. This multiplication of performative contexts exacerbates rather than ameliorates well-documented inequalities structuring cultural and creative work. Those lacking economic resources, cultural capital, or time to master platform logics find themselves increasingly marginalized, while established hierarchies of recognition reproduce themselves through new digital architectures.

By reshaping the organization of labor, collaboration, distribution, legitimacy, and even the artistic self, digital technologies are not just background tools but constitutive of cultural production itself. Their impact is central rather than incidental, altering both production and consumption patterns, as they open new avenues of evaluation, certification, and recognition. These shifts underscore that technological disruption is never only about novelty; it is also about the reconfiguration of existing practices and the redefinition of what counts as valuable in cultural industries. In all these accounts, technological disruption reveals that after a short period of destabilization – as ways of doing things, vocabularies, and tools are transformed – what follows is not "anything goes," democratic horizontality, or the "Wild West" fantasy of disruption discourse. Instead, we see the constant work of agents to restabilize what has been unsettled. To continue this line of inquiry, the next section turns to the repair and maintenance carried out behind the scenes, the "invisible labor" that sustains infrastructures.

The Invisible Labor of Maintenance and Repair

The infrastructural foundation of creativity described throughout this chapter emerges through historical processes of co-evolution between tools, work routines, and organizational forms: infrastructures must share enough to make participants part of a common world while leaving space for incremental change (Star and Ruhdeler, 1996). Creative communities develop through negotiated agreements about conventions – file formats, collaboration protocols, aesthetic standards – that become transparent to practitioners even as they fundamentally structure what can be made and how. These conventions extend far beyond any single creative site, learned through membership in communities of practice where newcomers gradually internalize the invisible rules that govern creative production.

Making sense of such networks requires examining collaboration while distinguishing the symmetry and asymmetry of the elements that sustain it. If the sociology of culture highlighted support personnel, the literature on scientific innovation has focused on the invisible labor (Star and Strauss, 1999) that makes science possible. In a foundational text for this perspective, Shapin (1989) makes the technician central because technicians embody the material, embodied, and tacit dimensions of knowledge scientists depend on but rarely foreground. Scientific work, he shows, is never reducible to theory, experimental design, or the published paper; it also relies on skilled hands that prepare specimens, maintain instruments, and execute procedures with a precision and consistency that make results trustworthy. Technicians stabilize the infrastructures of science – its laboratories, machines, and daily routines – by providing expertise less visible in the credit economy of authorship but essential to reproducibility and credibility. In *Leviathan and the Air-Pump* (Shapin and Schaffer, 1985), this point is clear: Boyle's air-pump experiments required assistants and instrument-makers whose efforts ensured the pump functioned, yet whose presence was obscured in the textual conventions of experimental reports. The credibility of Boyle's "matters of fact" rested on a material apparatus that could not be built, maintained, or operated without this labor, revealing that epistemic authority itself depended on unacknowledged technical work. In later essays, Shapin makes the claim explicit, presenting the technician as a paradigmatic figure who reveals the hidden social organization of science by sustaining instruments, enacting tacit practices, and keeping laboratories running.

Infrastructures reveal themselves primarily through breakdown and repair: when software crashes, supply chains fail, or established conventions no longer serve emerging needs. Maintenance is not marginal or exceptional; it is the quiet condition of possibility for any "normal" cultural order. It is the repair and maintenance work that ensures the flow of cultural objects (Jackson, 2014). For scholars of this perspective, these dynamics are revealed through infrastructural inversion (Bowker and Star, 1999), which uncovers the paradoxical centrality of support personnel in fostering innovation and producing culture. One example comes from Claudio Benzecry (2022), which shows the invisible labor of technicians, production managers, and fit models in stabilizing the global production of shoes designed and developed between New York and Dongguan, China. Fit models are women whose foot measurements approximate the perfect standard for size 6, the base used to scale all other sizes; they generate a last – a mechanical form shaped like a foot – around which the shoe is built. They also learn the qualities of materials and provide their own assessments. Though secondary to technicians and designers, because no foot is perfectly standard (there will almost always be a deviation among the twelve measuring points the industry uses), the entire infrastructure of shoemaking is recalibrated around these small deviations – sometimes a pronation, sometimes the toe sweep, or an arch without the proper curve.

Although it might seem peripheral, the fit model's role is central to shoe design and production infrastructure, functioning as a stabilizing actor that holds the entire network together. Every sample room has a designated model whose foot provides the reference point through which designers, technicians, and production managers calibrate their work. The process is so standardized that even substitutions must be formally communicated, lest the smallest deviation alter the system's function. The fit model's presence is not incidental but infrastructural – a seemingly minor element that enables distant actors to align their understanding of what they are examining, whether a spec sheet, prototype, or photograph. The paradox is that while no foot is perfect, the industry depends on treating one set of measurements and embodied reactions as universal, adapting entire infrastructures around the quirks of a particular fit model. Far from passive, fit models must train their bodies and senses, learning to speak on behalf of their feet as spokespersons for imagined consumers thousands of miles away. Their departure – and replacement – can be traumatic to the system, revealing how much is at stake in what otherwise appears secondary. Positioned as both subject and object, mannequin and megaphone, tastemaker and technician's echo, they embody paradoxical expertise that is simultaneously indispensable and subordinated, their value resting on a fragile balance of gender, bodily standardization, and learned responsiveness that stabilizes a global production network.

Beyond illustrating the work of repair and maintenance of invisible labor, fit models exemplify the power of inertia, their measurements fully accounted for in every design step. A model's resignation unleashes major concerns about replacement and how much work calibrating the entire infrastructure to new measurements would require. In the next section, we begin by discussing what this "power of inertia" is.

Art from Start to Finish: Process, Inertia, and Stabilization

We have meandered in the book so far between science and art, showing in one case the collective activity behind discovery, and in the other the collective activity behind creation (Shapin, 2018). Until the late twentieth century (Becker, 1995; Hennion and Latour, 1993), scholarly discussions about science and about art and culture drew from different traditions. As we saw in the previous chapter, cultural sociology emphasized primarily contextual and organizational factors to explain creativity; social studies of science and technology, conversely, made standards, devices, and mediation processes central to the endeavor. The following two decades made objects (Griswold et al., 2013; McDonnell, 2016, 2023; Molotch, 2003; Rose-Greenland, 2021) an important focus of contemporary cultural sociology.

In a follow-up elaboration of his celebrated *Art Worlds*, Becker (1995) focused on the stability and duration of certain artistic organizations by making explicit what he called "the power of inertia" and the barriers it presented to creativity, trafficking concepts between STS and the art worlds perspective. He introduced the concept of "package," which refers to a cluster of conventions, tools, procedures, and assumptions linked together such that once one is in place, the others follow almost automatically. Becker argues that change in art worlds is often difficult not just because of vested interests or active resistance, but because practices, technologies, and expectations are organized into packages with strong internal coherence. For example, in analog photography, the dimensions of negatives, enlargers, and paper are standardized together; changing one would require changing them all, which rarely happens.

Harvey Molotch's (2003) *Where Stuff Comes From* extends the analysis of cultural production by highlighting the importance of standards, infrastructures, and the coordination of diverse actors in shaping what cultural goods can be. His discussion of everyday objects – such as toilets, faucets, and other bathroom fixtures – reveals that design and production are not solely artistic or commercial decisions but are deeply structured by technical protocols, industrial standards, and regulatory frameworks. The physical form of these goods – their dimensions, materials, and modes of operation – emerges from negotiations among engineers, designers, manufacturers, and consumers, which in turn determine how the objects function, how they fit into domestic spaces, and how they signify taste or modernity. By unpacking the infrastructural and institutional foundations of such material forms, Molotch shows how cultural production is inextricably bound to material constraints that standardize what can be imagined, produced, and disseminated across industries.

A few years later, Becker, Faulkner, and Kirshenblatt-Gimblett (2006) edited *Art from Start to Finish*, an important book that made the artwork a key actor in the drama of its own making, emphasizing that materials and the media of art are central to explaining how creativity happens. The edited multidisciplinary volume also argued that a work of art contains and embodies everything that happened in its making and how it became finalized or stabilized. Much like in the laboratory studies at the chapter's beginning, tracing the process from start to finish has become a fruitful strategy for understanding cultural creation.

In *Art from Start to Finish*, the central claim is that cultural objects are, at once, "things that are many things": sketches, drafts, rehearsals, finished works, and the fragments or detours surrounding them. The longitudinal perspective the editors adopt turns time into a substantive dimension in the creation, production, and reception of art, reminding us that "finishing" is never a natural state but a negotiated resolution. From this angle, examining work-in-progress is not a curiosity but a method, allowing us to glimpse how training occurs, how autonomy is claimed in relation to constraints, and how uncertainty and variability become motivating conditions for participation in artistic life.

Menger's (2006, 2014) discussion of Rodin's sculpture exemplifies the project of studying art from beginning to end as movement toward stabilization, rather than as production of a naturally bounded object. For Menger, the interest lies not in treating the finished sculpture as a self-evident masterpiece, but in reconstructing the contingencies, trials, and choices through which it came to acquire its form and its status. The successive drafts, fragments, and recombinations of Rodin's work reveal a process where boundaries between preparation and completion remain open, and where the recognition of the work as "finished" is the result of negotiations between artist, material, institutions, and audiences. What eventually appears as a unified object is better understood as the stabilization of a complex trajectory – a trajectory marked by uncertainty, iteration, and the interplay of creative intention and external validation.

This insight extends to the idea that cultural objects emerge in and across distinct fields – artistic, economic, and institutional – where contingency continually meets intention. Epistemologically and ontologically, then, a work is not a singular entity but an assemblage of materials, practices, and relations that only later appear stabilized. Menger highlights the growing fascination with sketches, drafts, and fragments, where audiences seek to glimpse "what might have been," and in doing so theorizes that unfinished and discarded elements of the creative process provide a privileged window onto how the artist talks to himself, how intention works, and how provisional decisions come, eventually, to count as the final piece. In treating the sculpture less as a completed masterpiece and more as a problem to be solved through repeated trials, Menger shows that the distinctiveness of Rodin's work lay in the iterative processes and working logics – decisions made, abandoned, and remade – that crystallized into what would later be recognized as "the finished piece."

Skill acquisition runs through other case studies, revealing that becoming an artist is not about arriving at innate mastery but about learning to navigate uncertainty with available resources. Santana-Acuña's (2020) analysis of Gabriel García Márquez makes this explicit, showing how the novelist learned to write not only by drafting fiction but by working in advertising and movie scripts, where concision, pacing, and crafting memorable scenes became practical skills he later transposed into the density and rhythm of his novels. García Márquez's eventual literary style was thus the outcome of cumulative training across domains, where each context – commercial copywriting, cinematic narrative, editorial feedback – functioned as a site of apprenticeship.

A more contemporary study from this perspective, Hannah Wohl's research (2021) on the New York City art market from the point of view of artists navigating it, shows how it is not merely a site of exchange but a field that shapes experimentation, creativity, and career trajectories. She describes how artists negotiate constant tension between the radical uncertainty that defines contemporary art and the inertia of style, aesthetic visions, and long-term projects of the self, which demand consistency for recognition. The market rewards recognizable signatures, yet artists must continue experimenting to sustain credibility as innovators, creating delicate balance between novelty and coherence. Materiality plays a crucial role in this process: the specific affordances and resistances of media both enable and constrain what an artist can do, while also signaling continuity to collectors and audiences. Temporality further complicates this picture, since the unfolding of careers, exhibition pacing, and the life cycle of artistic projects all influence when experimentation is viable and when consolidation is necessary. From the artist's vantage point, then, markets are not external pressures, but environments interwoven with creativity, structuring how risk, innovation, and consistency are managed over time.

Whether by examining how collaboration, the division of labor, and conventions are key dimensions in art creation, or their inverse – how these produce inertia and stability – this perspective emphasizes a focus on how standards, conventions, and devices redirect, constrain, and organize individual artistic trajectories.

Conclusion

One lesson from our emphasis on materiality in this chapter is that culture corrodes (Benzecry and Domínguez Rubio, 2018;

Keane, 2003; McDonnell, 2016). The materials through which we construct meaning are fragile: they chip away, malfunction, and decay, requiring ongoing repair, retrofitting, and repurposing. Monuments that seem timeless slowly erode, artworks that anchor our symbolic worlds fade and perish, and everyday objects that scaffold our identities wear out with use. Much of cultural life, then, is less about grand creation than about the humble tasks of keeping things intact – mending, maintaining, and stabilizing what is always in danger of falling apart. It is precisely the everyday labor of repair that keeps meaning legible and usable.

A second lesson is to notice how studies of science and art have slowly converged to adopt methods that trace discoveries and creations by examining the stabilization process generated by multiple actors, standards, and devices, whether a fit model, a lab technician, or measurement technology. This has led to shared insights across the study of culture and materiality. Understanding a work of art or scientific discovery requires following its complete biography as an active participant in a complex network of relationships, rather than as a passive object created by singular genius. The work emerges through collaborative processes involving not only the named artist or scientist but also secondary actors and invisible labor – the canvas makers and pigment grinders whose contributions remain unacknowledged, or the laboratory glassblowers, animal caretakers, and data processors whose work enables scientific breakthroughs. Materials and tools function as co-creators, with the properties of paint and resistance of marble actively shaping artistic outcomes, just as the precision of instruments, purity of chemical agents, and reliability of measurement devices determine experimental results. The artwork's career unfolds through stages of becoming, from conception to iterations and revisions, while scientific discoveries move from preliminary observations through peer review, replication, and institutional validation, each phase asking different things of its human and non-human collaborators. Circulation through studios, galleries, and markets reconstitutes the artwork's meaning, while scientific findings circulate through conferences, journals, and laboratories, gaining credibility and being transformed through citation and application. The question of when art or science truly "ends" becomes complex – at the artist's signature or scientist's publication, through institutional recognition, or eventual obsolescence? Finishing, numbering, and authenticating artworks parallels the peer review, standardization, and replication that stabilize scientific claims, revealing how stabilization is always provisional, maintained through documentation, conservation, and institutional support that keep identities coherent across time and space.

The literature on disruption has shown how in some cases what has been reorganized involves who controls the creative process (think of the producer Seabrook discusses); how much autonomy each agent in the creative process has (as with the sound engineers Siciliano studied); how much authorship can be attributed to the artist (the digital artworks in Domínguez Rubio's account, and how authorship claims are distributed in such artistic objects); how consumption patterns have been changed by news digitalization and the consequent subversion of previous journalistic production standards (as shown by Boczkowski, Christin, Petre); and how we find new key players in gatekeeping – algorithms themselves and the authoritative advice they provide (as seen in the examples advanced by Gillespie and Seaver).

The third lesson, then, is to understand that disruption can be sociologically scrutinized and made into smaller queries, better answered through the study of discrete dimensions in the sociology of culture – like evaluation, cooperation, certification, distribution – while recognizing that it should be nearly impossible to study culture without examining technological mediation and its agency in producing new aesthetic patterns. For a time, understanding taste meant tracing the categories and hierarchies that social groups and their actors – gatekeepers like experts or critics – produced and reproduced, alongside the consumption practices through which they were enacted. That remains necessary, but no longer suffices in an era of Spotify, TikTok, and Netflix.

4

How does Cognition Shape Creativity?

Introduction

The molten chocolate cake, a luxurious individual cake with a liquid chocolate center, served right out of the oven, was a fashionable dessert in the late 1990s and early 2000s. First introduced in high-end restaurants, it became so sought-after that few upscale restaurants dared not serve it. Like most cultural products, the cake began to trickle down to restaurants of lower status until its widespread popularity turned it into a cliché, making it less suitable for high-end establishments. As is often the case with cultural products, there is debate about who invented the molten chocolate cake: most accounts point to the New York City-based French chef Jean-Georges Vongerichten, who claims to have invented it in New York in 1987, but this account is disputed on the basis that a molten chocolate cake already existed in France in the early 1980s, invented by the renowned chef Michel Bras. Regardless, Vongerichten is widely considered to be responsible for the popularity of the dish in the United States, if not its invention.

How did he come up with this idea? Following classic accounts of creativity – like many we have explored in previous chapters – we may think that Vongerichten is gifted with a creative mind, that he was deliberately trying to come up with an original version of a classic chocolate cake, or that he was embedded in a social context that facilitated the ideation of novel products. As the story goes, though, the molten chocolate cake was the product of happenstance: Vongerichten took a chocolate sponge cake out of the oven too early, so the center of the cake was still liquid. This undoubtedly looked like a mistake, but the cake had good taste and an interesting texture. Thus was a creative new dessert brought to the world.

Stories such as this one are plentiful in cuisine as much as in the arts, sciences, and design. Traditional accounts of creativity have got us used to thinking about creativity as a purposeful endeavor, or about creative products as the outcome of extra-ordinary "*Aha!* moments." At the same time, these accounts often revolve around radical innovations (often referred to as Big-C creativity), but if we expand our view of creativity to include more subtle, gradual, everyday innovations (Small-c creativity) we will find that the creation of novel ideas follows a myriad of paths. Some of these paths entail purposeful efforts to innovate and analytical thinking, others follow heuristics, intuitions, happenstance and, as in the molten chocolate cake, even mistakes.

Whereas in previous chapters we looked at more classical sociological concerns, such as the role of social context, culture, institutions, and knowledge in creative communities, in this chapter we will turn to the more recent sociological interest in cognition to understand *how* exactly people come up with new ideas. To understand this, we need to move the analysis inside the mind and look into how cognitive processing works. This will require us to look to research in the cognitive sciences (writ large), including cognitive psychology and cognitive neuroscience, to gain an understanding of how the brain processes information. However, we know from the cognitive sciences that equating cognition to an information-processing machine is misleading, because our brains do not process information in a vacuum, as if they were computers. So we will look at the connection between the mind and the body in cognition, how thinking unfolds in social groups, as well as how the physical environment anchors cognition. Once we have gained an understanding of how cognition works, we will move on to how sociologists have examined these issues, looking into contributions from several subfields, including cognitive sociology, culture and cognition, and the sociology of the body and embodiment. Throughout, we will highlight cognitive research from sociology as well as other disciplines to shed light on how creativity works, both at the individual level and within groups.

In this chapter, our aim is to answer some key questions about how cognition shapes creativity. What kinds of cognitive processes do creators rely upon in their work? How do different cognitive processes facilitate or hinder creativity? Is there evidence of a relationship between particular cognitive processes and creativity? What role does the body play in creative thinking? How does working with others inform creative thinking? And how does the physical environment shape creative thinking? Because we cannot explore the role of cognition in creativity without considering how people undertake new actions and create new things, we will begin with a brief discussion of how social scientists have thought about the relationship between cognition and action.

Theories of Action

Sociological theories have done much more to account for people's tendency to reproduce established patterns of thought and action than to offer good explanations of how and when people may engage in novel types of action. Two theories of action merit special attention for our discussion, namely Bourdieu's theory, and the work of American pragmatism, particularly the classic work of John Dewey ([1922] 2002) and the more contemporary version of Hans Joas (1996), for their focus on the explanation of creative action. While we introduced Bourdieu in chapter two, here we will zoom in on his theorization of action, rather than his work on fields of cultural production. Given sociology's general emphasis on constraints, we will begin with Bourdieu, who arguably had more to say about the habitual nature of thinking and action than the opposite, and then look into what may lead people to act creatively.

The notion that people regularly undertake routine actions and that, over time, such actions turn into habits – that is, actions that do not require much thought to be accomplished – is not new. But the study of routine actions, or practices, acquired a central place in sociology and anthropology in the late 1970s and early 1980s (Ortner, 1984). There were different scholars working under the label of "practice theory," including Bourdieu. His concept of habitus is a prime example of this perspective, capturing the automatic nature of much thought and action, and the consequent tendency for people to constantly reproduce habits and, in turn, social structures. The habitus, for Bourdieu, is a mental schema for perception and action that guides individuals in their apprehension of the social world and choosing paths of action without much conscious awareness. It is precisely Bourdieu's attention to mental schemas that has turned him into a central figure in the sociological study of culture and cognition, as we will see later in this chapter.

American pragmatism – a group that includes William James, Charles S. Peirce, George H. Mead, and John Dewey – has also gained influence in the sociological study of cognition due to their early interest in thinking and its connection to habits. Of all the pragmatists, Dewey (e.g., ([1922] 2002) wrote most extensively about habits and creativity. Not unlike Bourdieu, he emphasized the weight of habits in action, but he was more interested in figuring out what might lead people to act creatively. For pragmatists, all action arises out of a tension between routine action and creative reactions. This is not a rare occurrence, in their view, because everyday life always presents problems or new situations, and people need to be creative to respond to novel situations. Pragmatists view people as problem-solvers – i.e., we constantly face situations that require solutions – and see this as a core component of action and, what is more, the basis of creativity (see Joas, 1996: 126, 129).

The pragmatist understanding of action thus serves as an important corrective to the conception of creativity in two ways: one, creativity is not seen as the production of something completely novel, and therefore a rare, exceptional occurrence; two, creativity need not be opposed to automatic habits, but rather understood to be facilitated by the latter. Automatic habits indeed serve as the foundation for creativity, according to pragmatists.

Moreover, creative solutions to problems themselves become new types of action and, over time, habits. Some scholars go further in the attempt to bring together habits and creativity. Benjamin Dalton (2004), for instance, argues that creative action should not be reduced to a response to problems. He notes Dewey's ([1922] 2002: 40–1) understanding of habits as an "ordering or systematization of minor elements of action; which is projective, dynamic in quality, ready for overt manifestation." Dalton (2004: 609) astutely notes that artistic work demonstrates the problems with the dichotomic view of habitual and creative action, because creativity is not a response to problems in artistic work but an inherent, and routine, part of it.

Dual Process Models of Cognition

The tension between habits and creative action central to theories of action has continued to shape sociology, and has been taken up by sociologists studying cognition in recent years, who build on those early theories with knowledge from the cognitive sciences. One of the central mechanisms through which sociologists in this line of work have come to explain how thinking informs action is through the concept of cognitive schemas, first made central by Bourdieu. Because cognitive schemas work without conscious awareness, increasing attention to cognitive schemas in the sociological literature has led to a renewed emphasis of automatic thinking and habitual action.

But sociologists are not the only ones to assume that the bulk of cognition and action is habitual and automatic. There is consensus in the cognitive sciences that the bulk of cognition is automatic and deliberate thought relied upon more sparingly, because it requires mental resources that are scarce (e.g., Bargh et al., 2012). This has led to the formulation of dual process models, first developed in cognitive and social psychology, which posit that there are two basic modes of cognitive processing, the most common being autonomous (Type 1), and the other requiring controlled attention (Type 2). Type 1 processing is considered autonomous because it does not require the use of working memory, and is therefore often nonconscious and fast, whereas Type 2 processing generally involves conscious thought and is therefore slower (see Evans and Stanovich, 2013).

One particular type of dual process model has been imported into sociology (see Vaisey, 2009), what is termed the default-interventionist model (e.g., Haidt, 2001). This model posits the relationship between the two types of cognition in especially dualistic terms, with Type 1 cognition operating as the default mode, and Type 2 cognition taking over only when the other one proves ineffective. In the cognitive psychology literature, however, there are different dual process models that posit a less dualistic relationship between the two types of cognition (see, for example, Bago and De Neys, 2020; Pennycook et al., 2015; Sloman, 1996). Dual process models have gained increasing influence in sociology, not least because their core assumptions are consistent with well-established theories of action, including those of Bourdieu and Dewey, with their dualistic relationship between creativity and habitual action.

Arguably, one of the chief outcomes of the sociological dual process model has been an increasing emphasis on the weight of habits and automatic thinking and – an important point for our concerns here – an accompanying de-emphasis of people's tendency to think deliberately and act creatively. To the extent that Type 2 cognition is the kind of thinking that can break from habits and is naturally seen as the basis for creativity, creative action will be seen as a rare occurrence. Another significant implication of dual process models is that they place creativity squarely in the brain, reduced to the mental operations of analytical thinking. Creative thinking – or even automatic thinking – is rarely examined in its connections with the physical body. We thus turn to the role of the body in cognition and creativity next.

The Brain and the Body

How is it that the body takes part in thinking? And how can it help creativity? The body has entered cultural sociology largely through the notion of embodiment, a concept used to capture knowledge that is "stored in the body." Simply put, this is knowledge that may have been learned formally (e.g., piano lessons) or informally (e.g., proper ways to greet friends and acquaintances) but that, over repeated use, turns into implicit knowledge so deeply internalized as to feel like second nature (see Bourdieu, [1980] 1990; Wacquant, 2004). Though this concept can be traced back to Marcel Mauss' ([1934] 1973) theorizing of the techniques of the body, it is largely through Bourdieu that the notion of embodiment gained prominence in sociology. Bourdieu, however, used this concept in a specific manner, as one of the three types of cultural capital. In contrast to objectified cultural capital (e.g., your vinyl collection) or institutionalized cultural capital (e.g., your university degree), embodied cultural capital comprises the kinds of perceptions, skills, and knowledge that take time to acquire and become "long-lasting dispositions of the mind and body" (Bourdieu, 1986: 243).

This concept has been used widely in the sociology of culture, from ethnographic investigations into the acquisition of physical skills such as boxing (Wacquant, 2004) to work on the embodied nature of cognition (e.g., Ignatow, 2007). In general, though, sociological research on embodied cognition features the body in a fairly abstract manner, largely as the (abstract) receptacle for implicit knowledge, not as a physical entity that interacts with the mind in the process of thinking (but see Cerulo, 2018).

In the cognitive sciences, an interdisciplinary approach has coalesced to produce theories of embodied cognition (see Clark, 1997). This approach places the body as central in thinking, sensitive not only to the body's function as a receptacle for implicit knowledge, but also to its sensorial capacities (the ability to see, hear, smell, taste, touch) and emotions, which it considers intrinsic to thinking. The embodied cognition approach, along with related perspectives such as extended cognition and distributed cognition (Clark and Chalmers, 1998; Hutchins, 1995), also embeds thinking in the environment, finding both the social and physical environments to be key in processing information. This approach has emphasized the role of bodily and sensory experience in the mental representation of knowledge, even when it comes to abstract and conceptual thinking. One of the strongest lines of research in this area is what is called embodied simulation (Barsalou, 1999; Clark, 1999), which is particularly relevant to creativity.

Embodied simulation has to do with the capacity to mentally simulate sensorimotor experiences (e.g., eating ice cream), whether you may or may not have had the experience in the past. That is, it may entail the memory or the imagination of the experience, or a combination thereof. Research shows that embodied simulation involves not only mental imagination (i.e., picturing a tub of ice cream) but also the sensorial feeling elicited by the experience (i.e., sensing the coldness and creamy texture of the ice cream, tasting its rich flavor). This means that bodily and sensory sensations are inherently connected to the mental representation of an experience, and therefore that they work in tandem not only to re-experience previous events and stored knowledge, but also to conceptualize and envision new experiences. And this is precisely why this mechanism is particularly relevant to creativity. Whereas creativity is typically depicted as a eureka moment, or the outcome of the mental manipulation of symbolic representations (e.g., Farrell, 2001; Gross, 2008; Runco, 2014), the embodied simulation perspective makes a strong case against viewing mental representations as dissociated from bodily or sensory experience and ignoring the role of the body and the senses in the creation of new ideas (see Leschziner and Brett, 2019: 348). Scholars have also argued against the tendency to isolate the manipulation of symbolic representations from the environment, to which we turn next.

The Physical Environment

Famous stories (or legends) about innovative scientists and artists often highlight how the physical surroundings contributed to the "*Aha!* moment" that gave birth to a new discovery or artistic style. Among the most famous ones is the apple that fell on Isaac Newton's head and led him to conceive of the law of gravity, or Archimedes discovering the principle of buoyancy (the so-called Archimedes' principle) when he went for a bath and, upon submerging his body in the water, water spilled out of the bathtub, producing the scientific breakthrough that the amount of spilled-out liquid was equal to the body's volume. The art world is perhaps even more filled with stories about the physical environment's influence on artistic styles. Painting, being so inherently connected to light, gives us plenty of examples. Among the most famous is the case of Vincent van Gogh's artistic style being influenced by the bright and warm light in the south of France, where he resided in the last few years of his life.

However, when it comes to more prosaic examples of creativity (e.g., a manager trying to improve profits, or a social scientist outlining ideas for a new research project) the regular attributes of the physical environment rarely feature as a key component of thinking. That is, we may think of the role of the environment in special events and extra-ordinary circumstances – i.e., a new context, an abrupt change – but not so much in the ways in which the stable environment regularly informs cognition. But the literature offers several perspectives to analyze the ways in which the social and physical environment anchors cognition, including situated cognition (Lave, 1988), distributed cognition (Hutchins, 1995), and extended cognition (Clark and Chalmers, 1998).

If thinking is typically considered an activity that happens (only) inside the brain, Andy Clark and David Chalmers (1998) insightfully note, it is because it tends to be associated with consciousness. To be sure, our hands have no consciousness, and neither does our physical environment. But to the extent that we believe that the bulk of thinking is *not* conscious, it is harder to sustain the boundary that separates the thinking that happens inside and outside the brain. Clark and Chalmers offer the instructive example of a person who relies on her working memory to find the Museum of Modern Art in New York City, and another person who relies on his notebook to find the museum. The mind and notebook strike us as two entities that cannot possibly be analogous, but Clark and Chalmers point out that they not only serve the same function, but also suffer from the same constraints: just as a notebook is not always accessible, neither is our working memory, for it is out of reach when we are sleeping, under the influence of alcohol, or when our brains are occupied with a cognitively onerous operation.

All these perspectives suggest that the traditional understanding of cognition is misguided, for it disregards the active role the physical environment plays in our thinking. But the literature reviewed in this section offers important lessons for the understanding of creativity. We will discuss the role of the environment later in this chapter and more at length in the following chapter. In the next section, we highlight research that sheds light on the relationship between making and thinking in creative work, a relationship that encompasses both the connection between mind and body, and mind and environment.

Social Cognition in Creative Work

The dichotomy between habitual action and creativity that is central to theories of action has shaped research on creativity in psychology as well as sociology, in some cases explicitly and in others implicitly (e.g., Davis, 1999: 166; Joas, 1996). From the early days of creativity theory in social psychology, creativity has been framed as the creation of something new that occurs by breaking away from habits and routine action (Ross and Glăveanu, 2023: 2). Indeed, habits have been seen as a constraint for or even impediment to creativity (e.g., Ibáñez de Aldecoa et al., 2021; Wood and Rünger, 2016).

More recently, however, some scholars have questioned the dichotomy between habitual action and creativity. Much like

Dalton (2004), whom we saw above, one of the major figures in contemporary research on creativity, the psychologist Vlad Glăveanu (2012), has been arguing for a reconsideration of this dichotomy. He notes that habitual action entails more creativity than is often assumed and, moreover, that habits are more important for creativity than is typically granted, a feature he captures with the notion of "habitual creativity." This refers to the regular adjustment of habitual action that happens as people respond to a constantly changing environment, which requires changing or combining routines (Glăveanu, 2012: 84). Looking at examples of work in the arts and crafts, Glăveanu (2012: 79) notes, shows that higher levels of creativity are only achieved through constant efforts to master technique and perfect the work. The archetypical example of this is jazz, where performances build on a back-and-forth between the repertoire and improvisation, an example famously elaborated by Becker (see Becker and Faulkner, 2009). The argument that habitual action is the necessary bedrock for, rather than impediment to, creativity has been supported by much creativity research in the arts and sciences (see Sawyer, 2006: 22). Nobel laurates, for instance, have been shown to have over twice as many publications as other top scientists (Simonton, 1988: 77), which suggests that the most innovative individuals are also the most productive – an accomplishment that would not be achieved without much routine action.

Habitual creativity is just one of three ideal types of creativity that Glăveanu (2012: 85–8) identifies, the others being improvisational and innovative, all three of which we can trace to existing bodies of work we have already encountered. Habitual creativity, referring to the regular type of creativity inherent to habitual action, appears in prominent sociological work such as Bourdieu's (1990) and Becker's (e.g., Becker and Faulkner, 2009), though it is rarely articulated in much detail (but see Dalton, 2004 for an exception). Improvisational creativity, for its part, arises as a response to problems or changing conditions that hinder habitual action and call for deliberation. This is a type of creativity that has to do with the process rather than the outcome of creativity (see Glăveanu, 2012: 86; Sawyer, 2000: 149). It has been the focus of attention of theories of action – in particular American pragmatism – and the literature on social cognition that builds on them. Lastly, innovative creativity involves a purposeful attempt to generate novel ways of dealing with those problems or changing conditions. It is represented in much of the research on creative work in sociology and psychology, with its focus on the (typically purposeful and novel) production of objects.

In the remainder of the chapter, we will review research on creativity from sociology and the cognitive sciences that focuses on the role of cognition, with attention to the main areas we highlighted above, including the relationship between habitual and purposeful action and implicit and deliberative thought; the mind and the body; and the mind and the environment.

Implicit and Analytic Cognition

In his classic book on creativity, Arthur Koestler (1964) outlined an overarching theory of creativity that homed in on the interdependence between creativity and habit. Writing decades before Glăveanu, Koestler did not have much sociological or cognitive research at his disposal, but his insights about how novel ideas come about are still in line with current knowledge. Koestler saw skills and habits as necessary conditions for creativity, but thought this was due to a unique process he called bisociation. Bisociation refers to individuals' capacity to associate ideas from two separate frames of thought, or matrices, to form a new matrix of meaning through analogies, comparison, and abstraction.

Koestler noted that many breakthroughs in science and the arts happened *after* a period of intensive deliberate activity. During such intense activity, the person often becomes single-mindedly focused on the activity, Koestler explained, such that the topic remains active in her mind when she steps away from that activity and is engaged in other pursuits with logical thought on pause. These conditions can prompt people to connect two frames of thought associated with the two distinct pursuits and come up with a new idea. The fusion between the two frames only happens,

Koestler notes, not just when the context provides the right conditions, but also when the person has the required skills and habits to lead to a discovery. Cognitive neuroscientists support Koestler's insights. They have generally confirmed the existence of what they call an "incubation effect," a period of subconscious cognition that typically precedes creative insights. Moreover, they have suggested that people who tend to engage in "mind wandering," with their thoughts moving away from a goal-driven and deliberate task toward unrelated topics, tend to be more creative (see Sawyer, 2011: 146).

The case of Archimedes (as well as that of Newton) perfectly exemplifies the process of bisociation, as Koestler himself has noted. Archimedes, we saw, had his breakthrough while taking a relaxing bath, where he associated his scholastic knowledge about measurements of weight and volume with his ordinary domestic experience of taking a bath. Koestler suggests that the two frames of thought were likely active in Archimedes' mind, but not on the same level of awareness. Most of us do not think consciously about what happens when we take a bath, and this was likely the case for Archimedes, Koestler points out, until the moment of bisociation led him to think explicitly about it. Implicit knowledge – gained through habitual action and skills – is thus necessary, along with conscious thought, for breakthroughs.

Current knowledge from the cognitive sciences offers an explanation to understand the cognitive mechanisms that make the breakthroughs described by Koestler happen. The sudden insight itself is what scholars refer to as an "*Aha!* moment" (Topolinski and Reber, 2010). An "*Aha!* moment" occurs when we suddenly come up with an idea through what we experience as an abrupt, easy, and unexpected insight, rather than a slow and deliberative process. What gives it that "*Aha!*" quality, psychologists point out, is not simply the quick and easy cognitive processing involved, but the positive affect that typically follows an insight, insofar as we have confidence in the insight (Topolinski and Reber, 2010: 404). The positive affect is triggered, not by our psychological traits, but by the quick and easy cognitive processing engaged – what psychologists call fluent processing. Psychologist Valerie Thompson

(2009) aptly calls this "feeling of rightness," or FOR, noting that the more fluent the cognitive process, the stronger the FOR will be. In turn, having a strong FOR makes us less likely to engage in analytic thinking to evaluate an idea we initially came up with through implicit cognition. It is important to note, however, that this says nothing about how good or useful the initial idea was, just that we feel confident about it.

Cognitive scientists also examine the neural mechanisms that underpin "*Aha!* moments" to explain how the sudden insights happen in the brain (e.g., Tik et al., 2018). Paul Thagard and Terrence Stewart (2011) used computer simulations to study the neural activity behind creative breakthroughs and found that the combination of previously unconnected mental representations that leads to creative ideas entails a process of convolution – i.e., turning existing neural patterns into new and useful ones. Producing new mental representations, they note, encompasses the neural binding of previously unconnected representations as well as new emotional bindings, which helps explain the "*Aha!*" experience. All these mental operations happen in parallel, with the brain regions dedicated to cognition, perception, and emotion activated concurrently. Most significantly, Thagard and Stewart (2011: 11) add that if the "*Aha!*" experience appears to be so enigmatic, it is because we do not have conscious access to the cognitive, perceptive, and emotional processes that make the experience what it is.

The "*Aha!*" experience is but one step in the creative process, a process that social and cognitive psychologists commonly view in a serial progression that unfolds through several phases, including preparation, incubation, insight, verification, evaluation, and elaboration (Sawyer, 2006; see also Amabile and Pillemer, 2012; Policastro, 1999). While they disagree on the specific phases, psychologists generally agree that creativity begins with the quick gestation of a vague idea that is assessed and refined through a set of cognitive operations typically going from implicit to analytical thinking. This progression is also represented in more sociologically inclined studies of historical figures in the arts and sciences (e.g., Farrell, 2001; Galenson, 2006).

The serial model of creativity is fairly standard, but some scholars counter the idea that creativity happens serially, through phases that involve *either* implicit *or* analytical thinking, arguing instead that varied types of thinking take place simultaneously in the creative process (e.g., Runco, 2006). A growing body of research on dual process models underscores that creativity *requires* the interaction between Type 1 and Type 2 cognition (Gabora and Ranjan, 2013; Nijstad et al., 2010; for a review, see Sowden et al., 2015), especially for the incubation and evaluation phases, which are typically associated with Type 1 and Type 2 cognition respectively. Andrew Pringle and Paul Sowden (2017) go further and suggest that the incubation and evaluation of an idea do not happen sequentially but in a back and forth that entails a constant shifting between implicit and analytic cognition. They call this "mode switching," wherein people are aware of the type of cognitive processing being engaged and are therefore more in control of their thinking, a key factor for creativity (Pringle and Sowden, 2017: 18).

While we reviewed a variety of perspectives on the creative process in this section, they all share a focus on mental processing to explain how creativity happens. This focus may seem obvious given how we typically think of creativity but, in the next section, we will find other scholars who shed light on how the body and the environment influence creativity.

The Mind and the Body

Much like the sociological literature on embodiment and the environment we reviewed above, studies of creativity that attend to these phenomena generally make reference to them in a largely abstract way. The body is typically treated as a repository of skills and knowledge, but rarely an active agent in the creative process. This understanding of the body was famously developed by Bourdieu (e.g., 2017), who was more interested in what he called the position-takings of agents than the craft of the creative work itself, as can be seen in his various studies of fields of cultural production, including his major studies on painting, literature, and academia (Bourdieu, 1984, 1992, 2017).

Other sociologists, however, have sought to understand the craft itself, with some attending to the bodily skills needed to get work done. For instance, Molotch (2003) examines how industrial designers come up with ideas for innovative products. To be sure, these professionals draw on a variety of sources to spark their creativity, but a significant source is their own practical (especially physical) experience using everyday objects. Molotch insightfully notes that many products are an extension of the human body: eyeglasses extend our eyes, scissors extend our hands, and smartphones extend our brains. It is therefore no surprise that the ordinary use of regular objects would inspire designers. Molotch gives the example of the floppy disk, a worthless antique at present but widely used not too long ago. How did the floppy disk acquire its dimensions? Because the person in charge had a coffee stirrer in his hand and thought that was a good size (Molotch, 2003: 43).

DeNora (2000) offers one of the most influential contributions to the analysis of the body in creative work. In her now classic work on music, she sets off by noting that scholarship about music either examines music scores as representations (in cultural studies or musicology) or the context of music production (in sociology), but rarely does it examine the performance or appropriation of music, what she calls *music acts*. She thus studies the performance of music as acts that convey capacities and social categories, often in embodied ways. In one of her famous case studies, DeNora (2002) shows how the arrival of Beethoven's music to Vienna, with its new physically aggressive (i.e., "masculine") performing style on the piano, closed doors for female piano players because it required an embodied style of performance that was at odds with the gendered norms of bodily comportment.

In a book aptly called *The Craftsman*, Richard Sennett (2008) sets out to explain how people learn a craft using a range of case studies, from pianists to chefs and glassblowers. He attends to the role of abilities, instructions, tools, and workshops. Hand skills are of course key in crafts, and Sennett zooms in on the bodily practices required to hone them. One of his main contentions is that all skills, whether physical or analytical, start as bodily practices, because the hand acquires knowledge from the sense of touch and movement involved in the regular practice of craft, and it is from this bodily knowledge that people hone skills (see also Moeran, 2014: 202–3).

These studies offer rich examples to begin to understand how bodily practices anchor and spur creativity, but the body's role is still relatively limited in them. Molotch looks at the body only indirectly. DeNora has a keener interest in bodily practices at the piano, but historical records of 1790–1810 Vienna provide little information about bodily practices in action. And while Sennett looks at bodily practices more closely, he is largely focused on training and hand skills and not creativity so much.

Some sociologists zoom in on the senses to understand how the body and the mind connect in creative work, making use of the concept of embodied simulation, which we encountered earlier in the chapter. For instance, Vanina Leschziner and Gordon Brett (2019) show how chefs draw on their sensory memory of foods and combine ideas from disparate sensory experiences to design novel dishes. This combination may include the sensory memory of a dish a chef once ate (e.g., the taste memory of slow-cooked meat, the experience of succulent vegetables in the mouth) with the *imagination* of a sensory experience of eating another vegetable, producing a simulation that blends the separate perceptual symbols to create an inventive dish (for a similar analysis of creativity that highlights the role of imagination, the body, and emotions, see Root-Bernstein and Root-Bernstein, 1999). In all, attention to embodiment in creativity shows how people create new objects, not only by mentally manipulating symbols stored in the brain, but also through the bodily and sensory experiences that are inseparable from the skills and knowledge involved in their work (see Leschziner and Brett, 2019: 349; see also Root-Bernstein, 2002).

Analysis of the connection between the mind and the body in creativity has also turned attention to the role of emotions (see Root-Bernstein and Root-Bernstein, 1999: 2–6). In sociology, however, the study of emotions and of cognition have remained largely separate (but see Summers-Effler, 2022 for an exception).

Emotions have been shown to regulate brain activity and push the brain to action (Franks, 2014: 267) and, in the realm of creativity research, they have been shown to spur creativity by generating *flow* (Csikszentmihalyi, 1996), or the state of deep concentration and absorption in an activity.

A seminal figure in this line of work, Collins (1998) began to formulate the connection between emotions and knowledge production in an ambitious study of intellectual change in philosophy, ranging from ancient times to the modern day, and from Asia and the Middle East to Europe, later developed into a major theory of *interaction ritual chains* (Collins, 2004). Drawing on Durkheim, Mead, and Goffman, Collins posits that interaction rituals have a critical function across all areas of social life because they provide people with emotional energy. Eminent scholars, who achieved their eminence thanks to their creativity and devotion to their work, get high degrees of emotional energy from their work, Collins points out. And they transmit their focus and energy to those with whom they interact, whether peers, rivals, or students. Two consequences follow from this, according to Collins (2004: 192): "creativity is contagious" and "eminence breeds eminence."

For Collins, therefore, the emotional energy that people obtain from their social interactions is a key factor in the production of creative ideas. Much like psychologists we discussed above, sociologists who study emotions and knowledge production observe that emotional states can elicit thoughts but also serve evaluative functions (Barbalet, 2011: 41). Confidence or trust, for instance, are considered "anticipatory emotions" (Kemper, 1978) that help assess the value of ideas, and lead to action.

The Mind and the Environment

Some sociologists examine how the physical environment generates a shared emotional context that helps the creation of ideas. John Parker and Edward Hackett (2012), for instance, suggest that socially and physically isolated locations help strengthen social ties and commitment to shared ideas among collaborators, fostering productivity and creativity. This approach has been applied to different cases, from innovation in freestyle BMX or bicycle MotoCross (Corte, 2013) to archeological excavation (Rose-Greenland, 2013). Fiona Rose-Greenland further notes that the physical and symbolic boundaries around a site create a shared understanding of the site as a privileged social space, one imbued with "epistemic virtues" (Gieryn, 2006: 5). She also points to the role of the body and emotions in collaborative work, including the use of embodied knowledge and sensory experience.

These sociological studies stand out in that, unlike much of the sociological literature, they do not take the environment as a passive background, even if their analysis of how the characteristics of the environment foster creativity is still relatively limited. The psychology and education literature has gone further in this regard, applying the distributed cognition perspective (Hutchins, 1995) to study how relations among people and objects shape creativity. Reijo Miettinen (2006) and R.K. Sawyer and Stacy DeZutter (2009) first proposed this approach, under the name distributed creativity, mostly focusing on the distribution of cognition among people. Sawyer and DeZutter illustrate the approach with a study of improvisation theater. In improv theater, the story that is produced and performed on stage is always the outcome of collaborative efforts among team members – or, in other words, distributed across team members. The authors draw on the concept of emergence, capturing how creativity emerges from the interaction of parts in a system. This emergent process is also analyzed in detail by sociologist Brett (2022) in an article that zooms in on three interactions at play in improv theater: between order and disruption, between automatic and deliberate cognition, and between performers. In the realm of open source in science, law, and education, Miettinen (2006) similarly illustrates the workings of distributed creativity.

It only took a few years until other scholars supplemented the distributed creativity approach with attention to materiality, shifting the analytic emphasis from relations among people to relations between people and objects. Glăveanu (2014: 9) points out that research on creativity generally dissociates the individual creator (or the individual brain) from the social, cultural, and material environment in which the creator is "not only surrounded by but actually immersed in" (Glăveanu, 2014: 2) and highlights the ways in which creative action is distributed among people, creations, locations, and times. Craftmanship has been a favored case study for those interested in the relationship between people, objects, affect, and tactile sensation and skills, an example of which we saw earlier with Sennett's work. Glăveanu (2014: 83) similarly investigates various crafts (e.g., Easter egg decoration, wooden bowl making), underscoring that craftwork cannot be reduced to a mental process because it is just as importantly a psychological and physical form of expression. Neither can it be reduced to a single person, he adds, even when the person works alone, because it is embedded in a long tradition that goes beyond any one person, immersed in the context of community life, with its habits, social and material relations (for a related perspective, see Moeran, 2014).

Along similar lines, Dylan van der Shyff et al. (2018) draw on the perspective of 4E cognition – an approach in the cognitive sciences that brings together embodied, embedded, enacted, and extended cognition – to investigate music improvisation in groups. This case study, much like Glăveanu's research, allows the authors to examine creative work immersed in a specific environment, shaped by the relationship between individuals and objects, the nature of group collaboration, and individual expression. Through their study, the authors underscore the "deeply adaptive relational nature of living cognitive systems" that shapes music performance and improvisation (van der Shyff et al., 2018: 5).

Glăveanu (2014: 83) asks a question about craftwork that can be extended to all creative work: where does creativity begin and where does it end? Does it begin when the creator sets off to work? When she readies her materials? Or prior to all this, when she learns about the craft? And does creativity end when the last bit of paint has been applied? Or when the work is out of the studio and shown to others? Or when it is sold? From the perspective of distributed creativity, there is no need to make a choice among all these stages in the creative process, Glăveanu suggests, as long as we pay close attention to the psychological, social, material, and temporal dimensions of action.

Conclusion

If creativity is the creation of new ideas or actions, it stands to reason that to explain how it works, we would need to look at how people come up with new ideas or lines of action. This chapter began to look into this question, first by gaining some knowledge of how the brain and mind work, and of how scholars have theorized the relationship between cognition and action, before moving on to research on creativity.

The study of cognition in creativity spans many disciplines across the social sciences, cognitive sciences, and humanities, and the literature is vast. This chapter paid special attention to the more recent cognitive research that challenges the mentalistic assumptions about creativity that permeate much of the scholarly and lay understanding of creativity. Most basically, these assumptions revolve around the idea that creativity is largely the outcome of an individual's mental processing of symbols. In addition, creativity is often assumed to be a purposeful endeavor, therefore one that hinges on deliberate cognition, or something that results from an extra-ordinary "*Aha!* moment." We considered a variety of cognitive processes whereby people have been shown to come up with new ideas, and followed in the footsteps of some recent perspectives in the cognitive sciences that examine how the physical body, social relationships, and the environment factor into the creation of new ideas.

Paying attention to this wider range of phenomena has better equipped us to understand fundamental aspects of creativity, including the varied ways through which people come up with new ideas, how "*Aha!* moments" occur, and the role of emotions in guiding cognition and the creation of new ideas. Thus, rather than focusing on just one phase in the creative process – whether the initial ideation or the revisions required to create something new – we sought to cover how cognition may shape every stage in a creative endeavor, from the initial insight that may lead to something new to the decision that we have a fully formed creative idea.

We learned that phenomena as varied as cognitive processing, embodied actions, the senses, emotions, social interactions, and the physical characteristics of the environment all come together to shape creativity. Few, if any, scholars can study all these phenomena in tandem. Indeed, the literature we reviewed generally looks at only some of these factors, shedding light on important dimensions of the creative process. What we can take from the disparate perspectives we encountered is a richer appreciation of the different cognitive processes that shape creativity; how cognition (rather than being insulated in the brain) interacts with the body; how creative thinking happens through interactions with other individuals; how the interaction with objects and the physical environment informs creative cognition; and the diverse ways through which the creation of new ideas comes about.

Going forward, people interested in research on creativity would do well to expand the toolkit used to explain creativity to incorporate a wider set of cognitive processes and dimensions. But to more thoroughly understand how people come up with new ideas and make innovative products, we need to look into how individuals obtain information that is instrumental for the creation of novel ideas, what kinds of structural conditions facilitate or constrain creativity, and how structural conditions affect the ways in which innovations will be perceived by others.

5

What is the Social Organization of Innovation?

Introduction

Impressionism, the distinctive artistic style that emerged in Paris in the 1860s, is perhaps the most popular pictorial style in history. Associated with painters such as Monet, Renoir, Pissarro, and Cézanne, it is characterized by small and visible brushstrokes, depictions of outdoor environments and everyday life activities, and keen attention to the changing characteristics of natural light. Its current widespread presence in popular culture and products belies the fact that Impressionism was once a radical movement that revolutionized painting and the art world. It transformed not only the techniques and subjects deemed appropriate for painting but also the social organization of artistic work. This included the evaluation of pictorial qualities, the sites where paintings were exhibited, and the structuring of artistic careers and reputations.

The early Impressionists flouted all the conventions of academic painting, a style that had shaped and dominated the French art world. Prior to their emergence, artists typically worked in studios and painted portraits, historical or religious themes, still life, or landscapes, using clearly defined shapes and invisible brushstrokes for realistic depictions. The Académie des Beaux-Art controlled the French art world, establishing accepted conventions for painting concerning both content and style. The Académie's annual show, the Salon de Paris, selected artists to exhibit through a jury that reinforced these conventions. Being selected for this show awarded artists with visibility, prestige, and potential commissions.

However, the Salon regularly refused many works submitted by the painters who came to be known as Impressionists. This tension peaked in 1863 when the Salon rejected a significant number of Impressionist paintings, including Manet's *Le Déjeuner sur l'herbe* ("Luncheon on the Grass"). This painting, depicting a modern scene with a naked woman and two clothed men having a picnic, was controversial for its contemporary realistic setting. As the story goes, Napoleon III created the Salon des Refusés (Salon of the Refused) so the public could see the works and judge for themselves. The new pictorial style thus gained visibility and attracted more visitors than the Salon de Paris. However, the Salon des Refusés did not become an annual event, so the Impressionists formed an association to exhibit their work independently and began selling through art dealers, a new occupation of that period.

Impressionism has been as prevalent in scholarship as it has in popular culture. Typically, its rise is explained through individual characteristics such as psychological traits, living conditions, or group dynamics (e.g., Farrell, 2001; Smee, 2016). Some scholars point to broader changes in the social organization of the arts that facilitated the rise of Impressionism. In their classic book, *Canvases and Careers*, Harrison White and Cynthia White (1965) argue that Impressionism entailed not only a new pictorial style but also a change in the institutional organization of the art world. The transition from the Academic system to the dealer-and-critic system meant that dealers and critics gained the power to shape artists' careers. White and White suggest societal changes, such as the increased number of painters and the growing bourgeoisie, interested in purchasing smaller and less formal paintings for their homes, prompted this transition. In addition, with the increase of professional artists, the Salon's organization around individual paintings became less effective. By contrast, art dealers, interested in developing lasting economic relationships with artists and promoting their reputations, focused on artists' careers.[1]

We know that artists, even the most solitary ones, are embedded in a social environment structured by norms, conventions, and social relations that constrain their work (see Becker, [1982] 2008). However, the social environment includes not only norms and conventions but also social networks through which ideas diffuse and status structures that influence creativity. These elements create an unequal distribution of ideas, as well as risks and rewards to creativity. Some network and status positions increase the chances that an idea or product will reach the attention of others and will be seen as creative and valuable.

Why do actors (individuals or organizations) innovate? Innovation requires more work and is riskier than producing conventional objects. However, innovation is often necessary to stand out in a competitive environment. In some fields, such as academic research, originality is a fundamental requirement (Guetzkow et al., 2004). But not everyone innovates to the same degree. Indeed, we often find a pattern to innovation within an organizational configuration.

We begin this chapter with research on the rise of Impressionism to illustrate the chapter's focus: the role of structural features in shaping creativity, with a focus on organizational and social network dimensions. We will explore Bourdieu's field theory and organizational behavior perspectives to understand how status and reputation affect creators' work and careers. Additionally, we will review social network analysis research to examine how people obtain information that leads to new ideas and novel products. And we will examine research that considers how space and place shape creative work, complementing the structural explanations of innovation patterns that are the focus of this chapter. Looking at all this research will show that novel ideas are not created equal. We will examine where in a social structure there is better access to information for novel products, who has incentives to innovate, which social positions bring rewards or penalties to innovation, and which attributes of a location are instrumental for the generation of new ideas.

Organizational Fields

Social scientists have recourse to an array of frameworks to explain how organizations shape creativity, but theories of fields have an especially prominent place in the sociological study of cultural production. What is specific about fields, relative to other conceptual frameworks for analyzing the role of the social environment?

A field is generally conceptualized as an organizational configuration in a particular area of activity (e.g., painting) that shapes people's actions through shared ideas and rules about the work, and a hierarchical structure wherein people are located by virtue of their standing in that area of activity. Fields are relatively autonomous from the larger social space, in that the rules that guide action therein and the status structure follow dynamics that are internal to the field (see Bourdieu, 1993). These ideas are of course most famously theorized by Bourdieu, but organizational perspectives such as the neo-institutionalism in sociology and organizational analysis (see DiMaggio and Powell, 1983) and its spinoffs, such as the strategic action fields perspective (Fligstein and McAdam, 2012), have formulated frameworks largely in line with those ideas.

As we saw in chapter two, for Bourdieu, people come to occupy social positions in the field based on the types and amount of capital they have, and choose lines of action by virtue of those social positions. Fields of cultural production are structured around two poles, an autonomous pole of "restricted production," geared toward other field members and possessing the highest symbolic value, and a heteronomous pole where cultural production is geared toward the mass market, which can bring in economic capital, but at the cost of symbolic capital (e.g., Bourdieu, 1992, 2017).[2] This structure has been adopted to analyze a variety of cultural fields. For instance, in her study of fashion modeling, Mears (2011) shows how producers use different conventions for selecting fashion models depending on their field location. Those located at the pole of restricted production, which in the case of fashion is editorial work (e.g., fashion magazines or fashion shows), look for models with an "edgy" look, seeking to appeal to high-end fashion producers. Conversely, those located at the pole of large-scale commercial production choose models with a look that will appeal to the middle class that constitutes the customer base.

For her part, Victoria Alexander (2018) extends Bourdieu's framework in an analysis of public funding for arts organizations in Britain. Unlike Bourdieu's focus on the encroachment of commercial forces upon fields of cultural production, she shows that it is state policies that have turned the arts into a more heteronomous sector. Her analysis shows that this occurred when the state required arts organizations to implement neoliberal business policies in exchange for funding.

Bourdieu (1993) laid out a few arguments about when and where innovative cultural production may arise in a field, with two distinct sources of innovation: one that originates within the field and the other outside of the field. Regarding the former, the explanation revolves around the distribution of risks and rewards to innovation in a field. As the argument goes, people who have high status, being already at the top of the field, have little incentive to innovate. Those who are new to the field and/or have low status, are in the opposite situation, for innovating can help them get recognition and move up in the field. In addition, if their innovations prove successful, they may transform the structure of the field. However, those with lower status face steeper constraints to innovation, because it is difficult to challenge high-status peers and the status quo they represent, as science studies have demonstrated (see Cao et al., 2022: 9).

Other perspectives on organizational fields present arguments largely in line with Bourdieu, even if they do not necessarily engage with his theory. In a very influential article, Damon Phillips and Ezra Zuckerman (2001), for instance, suggest that low-status actors in a field have high incentives and low risks to innovation, given that they have little to lose, whereas high-status actors have low risk because it takes a lot to fall from the top. But these authors go beyond Bourdieu in arguing that individuals who are least likely to innovate are those with middle status, because these actors are sufficiently embedded in a field to be invested in it (unlike low-status actors and/or new entrants), but do not have enough status to protect them from falling if their innovations prove unsuccessful (unlike high-status actors).

Regarding the effect of exogenous forces on a field (the second source of innovation), the rapid increase of potential field members is of particular note, as we already discussed in the chapter's opening, and Bourdieu demonstrated it in some of his major works. He showed, for instance, that the fast growth in the number of writers – from lower social origins, too – during the Second Empire prompted the formation of an autonomous literary field in the nineteenth century (Bourdieu, 1992), and that the rapid growth in the student population, and in turn lecturers, in French academia around 1968 transformed the structure of the academic field (Bourdieu, 1988). External forces, however, explain changes in the structure of a field but not the creative choices of artists, according to Bourdieu. The latter can only be explained by artists' trajectories and positions in a field (Bourdieu, 1992: 55), because these are the forces that guide creative choices.

An important component of theories of fields pertains to how people make choices about the products they make, a topic we have explored in the chapter on cognition. In short, we know that, for Bourdieu ([1980] 1990: 53), this happens through internalized dispositions, such that actors make choices that seem instrumentally adjusted to their probabilities of success even if they rarely occur through rational calculations. Organizational theories of fields share the assumption that people internalize schemas which guide action, an idea famously outlined by Paul DiMaggio and Walter Powell (1983) in one of the foundational articles of the neo-institutionalism in sociology and organizational analysis (for another foundational article on this perspective, see Meyer and Rowan, 1977). Neo-institutionalism underscores that people's need to gain legitimacy in a field is one of the key factors that drive action. This need leads people to imitate products that already exist in the field and, in the aggregate, produces isomorphism (DiMaggio and Powell, 1983).

Though Bourdieu's theory and organizational theories were

largely developed independently of each other, they share the assumption that much of action occurs through implicit cognition, and that this results in the reproduction of established ideas. This has made both theories of fields subject to the criticism that they can hardly explain innovation and change. From these critiques was born the strategic action fields perspective (Fligstein and McAdam, 2012), seeking to identify sources of both stability and change in fields, and chiefly geared toward the explanation of collective strategic action (Fligstein and McAdam, 2011: 2). The criticisms notwithstanding, the organizational literature has inspired a wealth of research on innovation, offering important insights into some of the organizational forces that shape innovation patterns.

Categories

A prominent line of organizational research that investigates how status shapes innovation patterns homes in on the constraints introduced by the categories whereby products are perceived and classified. It is generally assumed that, in any field, there is a set of categories through which products are evaluated, and people face pressures to produce objects that fit with those categories for those objects to be seen as legitimate options, what is referred to as the "categorical imperative" (see Zuckerman, 1999: 1399). But categories have been shown to play a more important role in some fields than others. Fields where there are intermediaries (such as critics) are one such case, because categories serve as useful heuristics to evaluate and recommend products, for intermediaries as much as for audiences. The case of films shows this clearly, both in critics' reviews which classify films in terms of genre, and in the very common tendency to typecast actors into a particular role (Zuckerman et al., 2003).

Research on categories has been applied to a host of other cultural fields, including film, music (van Venrooij and Schmutz, 2018), and cuisine (Rao et al., 2005). Hayagreeva Rao et al. (2005), for instance, examine how categories shaped culinary innovation in France. In an investigation of the rise of nouvelle cuisine in the 1970s, the authors argue that classical and nouvelle cuisine were two culinary styles seen as opposite in the 1970s in France, so a chef *either* made traditional French dishes *or* used innovative techniques and ingredients associated with nouvelle cuisine. Borrowing elements from the rival category brought in penalties in the form of negative reviews. However, we know that high-status actors generally face fewer penalties by innovating, and Rao et al. (2005: 969) indeed find that high-status chefs were the first to innovate in this period. This, in turn, helped erode the strong boundaries separating the two styles and paved the way for other chefs to blend elements from the two cuisines and innovate without the risk of negative reviews. The authors extend their findings to argue that in markets structured around two categories perceived as opposite (in other words, separated by strong symbolic boundaries), borrowing elements from the opposite category to make a product is rare, because it entails blending two styles seen as irreconcilable.

The strength of boundaries that separate different styles is thus critical for explaining innovation patterns. But few fields are structured around two opposite categories – think of the myriad music genres there are, or the multiple movie genres. Even the culinary field, whether in France or elsewhere, is often structured around a plethora of categories at present, including the many "ethnic" cuisines, modernist cuisine, Nordic cuisine, farm-to-table fare, and so on (Lane and Opazo, 2024; Leschziner, 2015). Organizational scholars have argued that more fragmented fields, where there are people working in diverse styles, with different norms and standards, have no single set of criteria for interpretation and evaluation. This facilitates people's ability to conceive novel ideas, the diffusion of those ideas, and the reception of innovative works. For instance, in a study of the rapid success of Cubism, the new artistic style created in the first decade of the twentieth century in France, Stoyan Sgourev (2013b) argues that there were ambiguous standards of evaluation in painting at the time that made it possible for artists to create a radically new artistic style and receive positive support for it. Artists' ability to create a new artistic style and success in doing so in turn deepened the fragmentation of the art market, which enabled the existence of market niches accommodating different styles.

Conformity and Originality

Though the ability to innovate may hinge upon the number of categories existing in an organizational field and how clearly defined they are, that ability is not infinite, since any innovative product needs to conform to an existing category to be viewed as a legitimate option on the market. Yet, too much conformity to an existing category is not desirable, either, because there is nothing for a product to stand out among the competition, so some degree of originality is needed. The fine balance that actors (individuals or organizations) must strike between conformity and originality has been remarked upon by a wide range of scholars, beginning with Georg Simmel (1904, 1950), and including major figures such as Richard Peterson (1997) and James March (1991).

The academic literature can sometimes be fairly abstract in writing about the balance between conformity and originality, though the question of how much of each makes the ideal balance to succeed on a market is one that people in creative occupations must grapple with in and through practice (see Leschziner, 2015). Some academics have thus sought to specify this balance. Zuckerman (2016), for instance, proposes a couple of dimensions to parse out the qualities of conformity and originality. He suggests a "two-stage valuation" approach to explain how actors manage the competing pressures toward conformity and differentiation. In the first phase, there is a process of categorization through which a product is evaluated (likely implicitly, without conscious awareness) as a viable option. This process is all about conforming to existing categories. In the second phase, products must be differentiated from others to stand out and be selected (Zuckerman, 2016: 191). Zuckerman (2016: 189) specifies that there are incentives to conform to existing categories "on most dimensions" and to differentiate "on a few."

From a different perspective, Peterson (1997) has noted that maintaining a balance between conformity and originality is important for actors to appear "authentic," a case he made in a study of country music. A degree of originality is required for actors not to give the impression that they are purely copying previous work, whether their own or someone else's. At the same time, straying too far from the styles they are associated with can make them appear "inauthentic," so any originality must be kept within bounds. Taylor Swift exemplifies this case. Making a name for herself in country music, only to leave this genre and move to pop, rock, electronic, indie folk, and various other genres with every subsequent album, has often led to the penalty of being perceived as "inauthentic," and resulted (along with other factors) in negative reviews of her albums.

Incumbents and Challengers

The social distribution of risks and rewards to innovation is arguably the most prominent explanation of innovation patterns among organizational approaches. But innovation patterns are not only accounted for by status positions. How long organizations have been around has been identified as another central attribute that explains organizations' capacities to innovate. Organizations are thus typically classified into incumbents and challengers, with the former being well established on a market and the latter being newcomers coming in with new ideas (see Fligstein, 2021: 276–8).

The two types of organizations have different strengths and weaknesses. While incumbents benefit enormously from their experience (since they can easily rely on knowledge and skills they have developed and mastered over the years), this makes them much less likely to innovate. Their lower propensity to innovate may be due to a few different reasons. First, we know that established ways of thinking can constrain the ability to think in novel ways. Second, organizations become associated with particular categories and cannot easily deviate from them without suffering a penalty. Third, organizations develop intra-organizational structures that make it harder to change how they do things. By contrast, new organizations have less accumulated knowledge and skills or well-developed infrastructure, which may slow them down in generating products. But this makes them more nimble and therefore better positioned to innovate.

Much like the balance between conformity and originality, scholars have noted that organizations require a combination of exploitation of their resources and exploration of new ones to succeed (see March, 1991). Whereas incumbents tend to exploit their accumulated knowledge and procedures, challengers are more likely to explore new ideas and procedures. Phillips (2013) illustrates this argument in his study of the early years of jazz in the recording industry (see also Phillips and Owens, 2004). The dominant incumbent record labels faced all sorts of hurdles to record the more radical innovations of jazz, including the illegitimacy of a music genre associated with African-American people, resistance from the elites that were their audiences, and the difficulties of recording a new genre with different characteristics (e.g., improvisation in the recording studio). Incumbent companies thus selected to record a kind of jazz that combined elements of the new genre with components they had experience with and, importantly, which already had legitimacy (such as orchestras and white musicians), and this allowed them to attain more success on the market than the more radically innovative type of jazz (Phillips and Owens, 2004: 292–3). This, in turn, imbued a music genre that was seen as lowbrow and illegitimate by social elites with legitimacy. We see here how the balance between exploitation and exploration allowed dominant incumbent record labels to succeed.

Other perspectives in organizational analysis have also noted that older organizations are less likely to innovate because they are less prone to risk-taking or are simply slower due to inertia itself (Hannan and Freeman, 1984; Hannan et al., 2004), or because they become more rigid (Becker et al., 2005). The age and seniority of people at the helm of organizations have also been highlighted as an important factor, with older leaders or those close to the end of their tenure less inclined to innovate (Barker and Mueller, 2002; Sgourev, 2013a). A longitudinal study of the opera repertoire at

New York City's Metropolitan Opera, for instance, shows the specific ways in which age and seniority in managerial roles predict innovation, with age associated with high-risk innovation and seniority with low-risk innovation (Sgourev, 2013a: 568).

Social Networks

Structural explanations of the factors that facilitate and constrain creativity and innovation go beyond the characteristics of organizations. Among the most influential bodies of work in this area is social network analysis (for an excellent overview of the literature on culture and networks, see McLean, 2016). Social network analysis offers a unique perspective and methods to investigate how social connections shape innovation patterns, zeroing in on types of social connections and how information travels through them. A few broad attributes of social networks are especially salient, including the overall structure of social connections in a group (i.e., the social network), the positions actors occupy within the overall structure (i.e., network positions), and the kinds of relationships actors have with others (i.e., social ties).

Social network scholars have offered a variety of arguments to explain how these different attributes facilitate (or hinder) innovation. The legacy of Mark Granovetter (1973), with his classic work on how information travels through different types of social ties (i.e., strong or weak), has been enormously influential in sociology at large and in the literature on social networks and creativity in particular (e.g., Perry-Smith, 2006). Another important argument in this area of research pertains to the structural position actors occupy in a network, and whether actors have social connections across different groups, which is generally thought to be more conducive to creative thinking (e.g., Burt, 2004). In all, research on social networks offers insights into how the amount and strength of a person's social ties, the centrality of a person's position in a network, and the density and cohesion of the social network facilitate or constrain creativity (e.g., Obstfeld, 2005; Uzzi and Spiro, 2005). We examine each of these arguments below.

Three main features of social networks have been most significant in research on creativity: (a) the strength of social connections, especially whether these are strong or weak (see Granovetter, 1973), (b) how central people are within a network of relations, which means the degree to which people have direct connections with all other actors in the network (see Perry-Smith, 2006), and (c) whether people have social ties with others within the same social group or across groups (Burt, 2004; Perry-Smith and Shalley, 2003).

In line with Granovetter's (1973: 1361) foundational work, the strength of ties is determined by the amount of time individuals who are socially connected spend together, the emotional intensity and intimacy of the relationship, and the reciprocity between people in the relationship. Traditionally, strong ties were thought to be the best conduits of information, given that these ties are with people we talk to the most often, and those we feel we can rely on. So much so, Granovetter points out, that most scholars only looked at strong ties. Such a focus not only ignored what kinds of benefits people may obtain from outside their primary groups, but also the structural relations between groups. More significantly, Granovetter maintained that the study of people's strong *and* weak interpersonal ties serves as a mechanism for sociology to explain how small-scale interactions connect with large-scale social structures.

Thus, what made Granovetter's work (1974) so famous was that, contrary to what had become taken-for-granted knowledge, he found that weak ties were better conduits of information than strong ties. Drawing on interpersonal data on how people obtain information about jobs, he showed that people were indeed more likely to get jobs thanks to weak ties – that is, through connections that go beyond people's social circles. Whereas those in our close social circles may offer us information we have already heard, people outside of them are more likely to give us access to more diverse information and therefore increase the chances that we get new information about potential jobs. This is what led Granovetter (1973) to develop the theory of "the strength of weak ties." The fundamental premise is grounded on the notion that a social network where people are connected through strong ties is likely to be dense – i.e., many people are connected to everyone in the network – and this network structure tends to produce what is referred to as redundant information, whereas weak ties give people access to nonredundant information (Perry-Smith and Shalley, 2003: 94).

If this argument explained how people obtain information about jobs, it is all the more important for explaining how people get information that can help them think creatively, a topic that was briefly addressed by Granovetter (1973: 1367–8, 1983: 214–20). Indeed, connections to people in different social circles, which expose individuals to more nonredundant information, have been consistently shown to facilitate creativity by giving people access to diverse information that is conducive to original thinking (Burt, 2004: 350; Granovetter, 1983: 215; Perry-Smith, 2006: 97; Perry-Smith and Shalley, 2003: 94). We will come back to this when we discuss Ronald Burt's (2004) influential research and theory of "structural holes."

Much research on social networks has examined the effect of network positions on creativity, zeroing in on the benefits and constraints associated with core and peripheral positions in a network. People have access to material and cultural resources through their social networks, and some network positions have been shown to provide better access to resources that can help individuals come up with novel ideas (e.g., Collins, 1998; Sgourev, 2013b). But network positions also vary in the visibility, status, and legitimacy they confer to individuals (Godart and Mears, 2009; Godart et al., 2020: 499), all of which are fundamental for people's creative ideas to become successful innovations.

As is often the case in any body of work, the arguments about the relationship between network ties and creativity can be contrasting (see Cattani et al., 2015: 78). Some posit that being at the core of a social network, where actors have connections to more people in the social group through personal ties and are therefore more cognizant of what group members are doing, gives actors better access to information, material resources, and symbolic resources such as legitimacy and status. People in core positions are thus able to recombine ideas from different areas of the network and, because they are perceived to have higher status, are likely to feel more comfortable taking risks and innovating (e.g., Collins, 1998; Perry-Smith and Shalley, 2003: 96–7).

By contrast, others maintain that actors in the periphery of a network tend to have connections to people in other groups which may give them access to more diverse and new information, which is important for innovation. In addition, being less deeply embedded in the network, individuals may be less cognitively constrained by ways of thinking and social norms shared by those at the network's core, so they are better able to recognize and value novel ideas, and make use of the ideas (Perry-Smith and Shalley, 2003: 98), all of which may facilitate their ability to think creatively (Cattani et al., 2015).

The most influential contribution from this literature is undoubtedly Burt's (2004) "structural holes" theory. Burt gathered a sizable dataset of opinions and behaviors from managers at a large electronics company to study who was likely to propose novel ideas and encounter a positive reception for the ideas. Through this data analysis, he shows that individuals who have social connections across social groups that are otherwise disconnected from each other (i.e., no other social tie connects the groups) have access to different ideas which they can introduce into their group, where they will be novel. Brokerage across disconnected social groups, what Burt calls structural holes, provides "vision advantage," and this is the central mechanism through which people obtain ideas that will be novel in their group (Burt, 2004: 351). This turns brokerage into social capital, and a powerful resource for people in organizations.

Burt has a particular conceptualization of creativity, which he states explicitly. He views creativity as an "import-export business," such that he is less interested in how new ideas are produced than in the value produced by new ideas (Burt, 2004: 388). To the extent that having connections across structural holes gives people access to different information and interpretations that are useful for coming up with valuable ideas, this makes people appear "gifted with creativity" (Burt, 2004: 388). Individuals do not need to come up with elaborate innovations to bring in valuable ideas to their group, he points out, but can simply recombine ideas from different groups, or even directly import ideas that may be old in other groups but new in their own circles (Burt, 2004; see also Godart et al., 2014). "An idea that is mundane in one group can be a valuable insight in another," Burt (2014: 388) writes to underscore the point.

Of course, it is one thing to come up with a new idea and have it recognized within one's company (Burt's object of study), and a whole different thing to turn this idea into an innovation that will succeed on the market. For this, producers need to get attention. Social network analysis shows that those social positions that present advantages in terms of access to divergent information may be unfavorable for getting attention, and vice versa. Being at the periphery, for instance, gives actors an advantage to think creatively, but it constrains them in their capacity to turn their novel ideas into successful innovations, given that their marginal position affords them less visibility and legitimacy, a point already made by Granovetter (1973: 1367) in his seminal work (see also Sgourev, 2013b). By contrast, actors at the core benefit from high visibility, status, and legitimacy, but are often constrained in their capacity to access novel information and think in ways that are out of sync with standardized ideas and norms (Burt, 2004).

So how do new ideas effectively turn into successful innovations? Some scholars have sought to reconcile what appear to be inconsistent arguments, including whether the core or the periphery give better access to novel ideas (see Cattani et al., 2015: 76–7; Sgourev, 2013b: 1601). Some suggest, for instance, that actors at the core and periphery of a network are likely to come up with different types of innovations, with those at the core more likely to recombine ideas and therefore generate incremental innovations, and those at the periphery more likely to conceive of more novel ideas and produce divergent innovations (Cattani et al., 2015; Perry-Smith and Shalley, 2003; Sgourev, 2013b).

Between the opposite network positions, some see a sweet spot placed between the benefits of peripheral positions and the advantages of the core, where actors may be ideally positioned to produce novel ideas *and* gain visibility and legitimacy, aptly termed "optimal marginality" (McLaughlin, 2001) or "optimal network structuration strategy" (Cattani et al., 2015; see also Godart et al., 2020: 499). Historical case studies of intellectuals and artists demonstrate the advantages of this optimal position, a phenomenon we clearly see in Neil McLaughlin's (2001) investigation of the career of the German-trained psychoanalyst and sociologist Erich Fromm, who moved to the US in the early 1930s, became a central member of the early Frankfurt School and had connections to various prestigious psychoanalytic and sociological institutes and circles, and moved to Mexico in the 1950s. Fromm also maintained a psychoanalytic practice and wrote books for the general public, with which he achieved great success. McLaughlin shows that while Fromm had connections to dominant psychoanalytic and sociological circles, he also maintained a critical distance from them, enabled in part by his involvement with disparate intellectual groups, his financial independence (thanks to his popular books and psychoanalytic practice), and later his physical distance from the intellectual elites in New York City. The balance between his involvement with mainstream ideas and groups and distance from them – what McLaughlin calls "optimal marginality" – allowed him to conceive of ideas that diverged from the core's orthodoxies, while also being sufficiently connected to the core to obtain material and symbolic resources for turning his ideas into finished products, receive attention for them, and gain legitimacy.

Gino Cattani et al. (2015) illustrate a similar phenomenon with the famous film director Stanley Kubrick, who moved to the UK after his success in Hollywood, and founded his own production company but maintained a critical connection with the Hollywood studio Warner Bros Pictures, which still distributed his films. Much like Fromm, Kubrick benefited from the connections with and distance from core people and organizations. In Cattani et al.'s (2015: 84) words: "In essence, the optimal network structuration strategy builds on the power of ties that cut across the boundaries of both social worlds allowing core actors to reach out to the fringe and so benefit from a peripheral partner's fresh perspective; and allowing peripheral actors, who lack the legitimacy and status necessary to gather attention around their own work, to build on the core partner's social clout to gain legitimacy."

Scholars have examined not only the causal relationship between network positions and innovation but also how the latter can alter an actor's network position. Jill Perry-Smith and Christina Shalley (2003: 90), for instance, note that when actors on the periphery produce groundbreaking innovations, they will move toward the network's core, where they will have access to more people and information, which will generate new creative ideas. The authors suggest that this cycle will go on until actors become too central, which will ultimately constrain their capacity to think creatively (Perry-Smith and Shalley, 2003: 90). Other scholars point out that this process may only apply to actors on the periphery who produce gradual innovations, because these make it easier (than groundbreaking innovations) to slowly move toward the center of the network. Sgourev (2013b: 1603) suggests this was the case of Impressionist painters, but not of more radically innovative artists, such as Cubists, who may have lacked the resources to attain visibility and legitimacy. Cubism, however, did attain rapid success, and this was only possible, argues Sgourev, due to the artistic field's ambiguity and fragmentation, as we discussed above. In analytical terms, this means that cases like Cubism can only be explained through a combined analysis of social networks and fields.

Collins' (1998) imposing historical study of philosophy is an exemplar of such a combined analysis for the investigation of patterns of intellectual production. Collins proposes three major factors that structure intellectual fields and shape intellectual production: the existence of intellectual groups, intergenerational chains, and rivalries among group members. A variety of mechanisms bring these factors together to explain creativity, chief among which is the principle of "eminence breeds eminence" (Collins, 1998: 68) that captures the tight networks that are common among eminent scholars, including contemporary and intergenerational networks, and with rivals as well as allies. Intellectual exchanges that happen through these networks create chains of "emotional energy" (see Collins, 1998: 23, 2004), which help produce intense focus of attention; such intense focus in turn strengthens emotional energy. Through his investigation of philosophers across a plethora of historical and geographic cases, Collins finds evidence of a positive association between the degree of eminence of philosophers, the likelihood of being students of eminent philosophers, the number of social connections with eminent peers, and the number of students eminent philosophers have. Only a few of these students will become eminent, due to the limits of what Collins (1998: 81) calls the intellectual attention space, which allows no more than six eminent figures, and more typically about three, at a given time. Lastly, Collins argues that the denser the social network among philosophers, the more influence their innovative work will have.

Space and Place

While the structural perspectives we have discussed in this chapter have provided enormous contributions to our understanding of patterns of creativity and innovation, they nonetheless maintain some limitations that are common to structural analyses. Social network analysis and theories of fields – and Bourdieu's theory in particular – have been criticized for having an abstract conceptualization of the social space, where social relations and social positions are abstractions rather than actual relationships between people or positions in physical space (Bottero and Crossley, 2011). So in this section we will look at scholarship that supplements structural approaches to creativity and innovation with a focused analysis of space and place, demonstrating that spatial characteristics go a long way in explaining what conditions facilitate innovation and where we are likely to find the most innovative artists and scientists (e.g., Hellmanzik, 2010; Oberlin and Gieryn, 2015; Powell et al., 2005).

Perhaps counterintuitively, the contemporary world makes it especially important to examine the role of space and place in creativity and innovation, since the rise of digital technologies has given way to a popular assumption that co-location and face-to-face interactions no longer matter when we can access information and communicate with people from almost anywhere in the world. Yet, research shows that location still matters for creativity and innovation, even in areas of cultural production that are highly globalized. Benzecry (2022), for instance, demonstrates this is the case with an ethnographic investigation of creative work in the shoe industry. While trend spotters, fashion designers, managers, technicians, factory floor workers, and shoe models may all reside in different locations across the globe and often communicate virtually, Benzecry shows that geographically bound clusters of expertise and sustained face-to-face interactions remain central to product design and development. For example, designers are concentrated in New York City, while sample rooms, production managers, technicians, fit models, and related support services are clustered in Dongguan, China – an organization that sustains the close entwinement of design and production. In Benzecry's (2022: 210) words: "The levels of interdependence and integration eventually crystallize into infrastructural inertia . . . that anchors – at least for some time – development, if not production, in place."

There is a vast literature on space and place and how they relate to urban development and innovation. This literature can be traced back to sociology's early days in the US with the pioneering work of the Chicago School of Sociology (see Park and Burgess, 1925), subsequently the enormously influential work of Jane Jacobs (1969), and in more recent times the scholarship in urban geography and urban economy, with Richard Florida's (2005) ideas about the "creative class" being among the most prominent. Much of this literature is more aimed at explaining urban and economic growth than the dynamics of creativity, so the latter often appears as an explanans rather than the explanandum. Below, we sketch out contributions from this body of work that pertain to our concern, namely how space and place shape creativity.

With her prolific work on urban development and economic growth, and deep belief in the role of cities for creativity, Jacobs is a preeminent figure in this literature. She theorized a general process that occurred in cities, wherein economic growth and creativity become deeply intertwined. She found that talented people often left their jobs in large organizations to create smaller organizations where they did similar work. These smaller organizations require new goods and services, and thereby generate new jobs and new small organizations to supply those goods and services (Jacobs, 1969: 97). While this involves unplanned and inefficient developments, Jacobs acknowledged, she also noted that it leads to positive outcomes such as diversification and innovation.

Allen Scott (2000) builds directly on Jacobs' ideas on the interrelationship between urban and economic growth and creativity. The production of cultural products, as we have already seen, depends on the type of work than can happen through direct personal contact and technology, and it is typically organized in dense networks of relatively small organizations interconnected through chains of supply and demand of goods and services. These networks, Scott points out, require a large local labor force with varied skills, but often offer unstable work (a phenomenon Menger [2014] described), so there is a constant search for new workers. This means that a large local availability of labor is highly beneficial. Local clustering thus becomes critical for areas of cultural production, so much so that Scott (2000: 12) goes on to suggest that "innovation, all else being equal, is likely to be a geometric function of the size of the relevant reference group."

Florida (2005: 32) credited Jacobs for identifying the unique capabilities of cities to attract creative people, and argued that creative people, in turn, help to usher in economic growth – an insight that is at the roots of his renowned "creative class" theory. This theory proposes that cities foster the development and clustering of creative occupations through a formula of three Ts: technology, talent, and tolerance. Of course, technology and the concentration of talent have long been highlighted as key, but Florida adds a critical emphasis on the importance of tolerance of diversity (specifically what he called the "gay index" to measure the concentration of same-sex couples).

In a well-known study of the creative economy in New York City, Elizabeth Currid-Halkett (2009) offers more insight into how local clustering matters for creativity. For one thing, she argues that the informal social exchanges that take place thanks to local clustering of different areas of cultural production in a city should be considered "the center of action" (Currid-Halkett, 2009: 89). The power of cities as hubs for creativity is not simply due to population density (though this is valuable for people to run into each other and have informal exchanges) but also to the diversity of skills that exist therein, and the ease with which cross-pollination can happen when people circulate through the same spaces. She shows this in her study, where designers, artists, musicians, and others she interviewed in New York City recounted how they constantly run into each other at informal events (e.g., art galleries, movie theaters, nightclubs, bars, and restaurants) and formal social events (e.g., gallery openings, industry parties). These places where creative people meet do not merely serve as sites for socializing, Currid-Halkett (2009: 95) shows, but are rather "nodes of creative exchange," where art and business are brought together. Creativity breeds creativity, she concludes, as "the concentration of creativity leads to greater chances of more creativity happening" (Currid-Halkett, 2009: 91).

Scholars who look closely into spatial organization within a city provide a fine-grained distinction about the clustering of organizations and creativity. For instance, Gregory Spencer (2015) suggests that, while the same cities and regions may attract areas of cultural production as well as science and technology industries, they do so through different mechanisms and with different outcomes. In a study of three major cities in Canada, Spencer (2015) shows that areas of cultural production tend to cluster in dense, mixed-use neighborhoods close to downtown, and science and technology industries are typically clustered in the suburbs, in low-density, single-use neighborhoods (Silicon Valley, in the US, is a prime example of this). For one thing, creative industries are often built on small organizations connected through large social networks, whereas science and technology industries generally have large organizations and smaller social networks, Spencer argues. This helps explain why the two types of industries tend to evolve geographically in disparate ways (Spencer, 2015: 886), with the former benefiting from the density and diversity of knowledge and information encountered in a central location and the latter from being in an area with specialized skills and, arguably, the easier availability of space.

The attributes of areas within cities have also been shown to influence urban economic development and creativity through what has been termed "social scenes" (for an extended analysis of the concept and its use in sociological research, see Silver and Clark, 2016). Daniel Silver et al. (2011) lay out the main principles of this perspective, arguing that local amenities (e.g., cafes, parks, music venues, shops) have a key role in defining the value and symbolic meanings of an urban scene. Amenities allow for different kinds of experiences (distinguished by the degree of legitimacy, authenticity, and theatricality they can afford) and, in turn, strongly shape the type of urban development and levels of innovation we will see there (Silver et al., 2011: 234). Conducting a quantitative analysis of these dimensions, along with other indicators of urban development, they find that social scenes have an economic effect in attracting skilled labor; scenes also have an effect by adding symbolic and affective value to what people do, connecting residents to their community, and to other residents dedicated to "the search for new ways of thinking and being" (Silver et al., 2011: 252). Areas that facilitate the feeling of a sense of place, they suggest, foster social ties that offer continuity, security, support, and trust, all of which are important for managing the uncertainty and instability associated with creative work (Silver et al., 2011: 253), an important point that adds a new dimension to the understanding of how place shapes creative work.

Attention to space and place has also been combined with the kinds of organizational and social networks perspectives we discussed in this chapter to show how geographic location informs knowledge production. Powell and colleagues (e.g., Owen-Smith and Powell, 2004; Powell et al., 2005), for instance, show how co-location shapes the biotechnological industry, perhaps unsurprisingly given how geographically clustered this industry is, both in the US and Europe. Owen-Smith and Powell (2004) demonstrate how the geographic agglomeration of all the organizations critical for the industry, including biotechnology firms, research universities, and venture capital firms, helps sustain high levels of innovation. Silicon Valley is, of course, a prime example of this (for the important role of venture capital firms in innovation in Silicon Valley, see Ferrary and Granovetter, 2009). Co-location facilitates the development of informal network channels through which firms can obtain information, increase visibility, and hire specialized staff (Owen-Smith and Powell, 2004: 7). Geographic clustering and its effects on innovation are not only typical of the biotechnology industry, but rather common to areas that are heavily reliant on new knowledge, which is best transmitted through informal local networks (Audretsch and Feldman, 1996).

Beyond industrial sectors, geographic clustering has also been shown to be common in artistic and intellectual fields, where informal knowledge is similarly key (Kelly and O'Hagan, 2007) and best shared through face-to-face interactions (Collins, 1998). Historical research provides a wealth of evidence of geographic clustering of artists and scientists (e.g., de Courson et al., 2023). Artists clustered in a location have been found to be more prolific than geographically isolated artists, a phenomenon that has been shown among renowned classical music composers in the eighteenth and nineteenth centuries (Borowiecki, 2013). Artists have also been shown to see higher prices for their art – for instance, in a study of early twentieth-century painters in Paris and New York (Hellmanzik, 2010).

From a different research tradition, Kathleen Oberlin and Thomas Gieryn (2015) similarly demonstrate the critical role of co-location for the emergence of artistic styles. Artistic schools, they note, are often labeled with the name of a geographic location, such as the School of Paris or Young British Artists (Oberlin and Gieryn, 2015: 20), which arguably indicates how much co-location matters for the development of something as innovative as an artistic school. Throughout the twentieth century, artists have been found to cluster not only in cities, but the same neighborhood, street, and even building, likely because this endows them with easy access to material, social, and cultural resources, which are critical for the development of new artistic schools and success of its members on the art market (Oberlin and Gieryn, 2015: 21,

25). Oberlin and Gieryn (2015: 22) highlight the critical role of co-location for the initial phase of development of an artistic style (for a similar argument, see Farrell, 2001), when a place affords meaning to the art produced therein, informing how the work will be viewed by critics and positioned on the art market (Oberlin and Gieryn, 2015: 24). Once an artistic school has acquired critical reputation and market success, co-location becomes less important for artists in that group, since the collective style is already well defined, and the spillover effects of co-presence therefore less needed (Oberlin and Gieryn, 2015: 29).

Places have been shown to influence creativity even through temporary travel (Hellmanzik, 2014). But all travel is not created equal when it comes to creativity. Surveys of painters from the Impressionist era to contemporary times show that temporary travel has a positive effect on artists' productivity and the value of their work particularly when artists travel to centers of artistic innovation (such as France and Germany in the early twentieth century and the US in the postwar period), where they can derive inspiration and benefit from spillover effects. By contrast, locations with high tourism, even those with valuable art history, such as Italy, appear to have no effect on productivity or valuation (Hellmanzik, 2014). Christiane Hellmanzik argues that it is not simply spillover effects that artists benefit from because the positive effects of travel lose significance over the twentieth century, as artistic styles move toward abstraction, which might indicate that the place itself may have been a source of inspiration for figurative art.

Science has also been found to benefit from co-location (e.g., Duede at al., 2024; Hollingsworth, 2000), though here, geographic and organizational effects are often conflated. Research on scientific innovation typically shows the benefits to collaboration across departments or institutes within the same university. J. Hollingsworth (2000), for instance, demonstrates that universities structured in such a way as to facilitate interactions among scholars from different disciplines tend to generate more innovative science, and indeed more Nobel prizes among faculty. Analyzing large bodies of data through computational methods, Eamon Duede et al. (2024: 11) similarly find that when scholars incorporate research done in other departments or units in their universities, their publications become more influential than publications that cite research from their own department or from other universities. What is more, the more intellectually distant the research they incorporate, the higher the influence of the publications.

Conclusion

In this chapter, we have looked at the influence of structural forces on creativity and innovation, with a focus on organizational perspectives and social network analyses given how prominent they have been in the study of creativity and innovation. Despite their analytical and methodological differences, theories of fields, organizational perspectives, and social network analysis share an explanatory focus on how the structure of relations among actors – whether individuals or organizations – shape patterns of creativity and innovation. Theories of fields and organizational perspectives take social relations to be relations between positions that actors occupy in the social space rather than actual relationships. This is not the case of social network analysis, as we saw, and it is indeed one reason why this approach productively complements organizational perspectives to explain innovation patterns. Whereas theories of fields and organizational perspectives are especially illuminating for understanding the distribution of incentives and constraints to innovation across status positions and their profound influence on patterns of innovation, social network analyses help explain how information travels through social connections and how different network structures and positions influence access to information and resources that can lead to the creation of novel ideas and success of innovative products.

Whether the social space is conceptualized as a status structure or a network structure, these perspectives demonstrate that there is an unequal distribution of conditions in the social space that facilitate or hinder innovation. The social space is generally an abstraction, a configuration that captures the positions of actors vis-à-vis one another, but rarely captures the physical characteristics of space. This is why we introduced literature that analyzes how space and place help explain where and when innovations arise, supplementing the structural explanations that are at the core of the chapter. In some cases, we were even able to see how the social and physical space influence each other and together shape innovation patterns.

It is worth drawing attention to a common attribute that is implicit in the structural perspectives we examined in this chapter, namely the conceptualization of innovation as the outcome of resources and extrinsic rewards. This is especially clear in theories of fields and organizational perspectives, where individuals and organizations are typically assumed to be in a quest to maximize benefits, typically to maintain or improve their social positions. Even the very existence of intellectual property law, and much of the legal scholarship supporting it, is premised on the assumption that incentives and rewards are necessary to stimulate people to innovate (see Johnson, 2012). The extrinsic rewards thought to drive actors to innovate include the potential to increase their prestige and status, improve their economic position, or further professional advancement. We discussed the role of intrinsic rewards and internal attributes driving creativity in previous chapters. As we move toward the concluding chapter of the book, we may want to bear all the different forces behind creativity and innovation in mind, and consider how to complement different approaches, lest we forget that creativity requires both actors with particular motivations and skills and social conditions that facilitate creative work.

6

Toward a Sociology of Creativity

Several years ago, one of us taught a fourth-year undergraduate seminar in creativity and innovation. Having been embedded in the creativity and innovation literature in the social sciences, we came to the first class equipped with some hopefully persuasive arguments about the importance of studying creativity and the need to look beyond the deeply ingrained sociological focus on constraints. We launched a lengthy argument about the fact that, despite the wide variety of social constraints that surely shape creative patterns, individuals do break away from those constraints and act in creative ways, and laid out the reasons why it is important to examine and analyze this. Students looked nonplussed, as if they did not understand why we were so insistent on a point that was so obvious.

This was an eye-opening moment, and it is illuminating because it shows the disjuncture between the lay understanding of creativity and the sociological approach. Students came to this seminar – in the early 2010s – with the clear impression that this moment in history was a high point for creativity, given that the development of Internet, smartphones, and social media made access to information, collaboration, the creation of cultural objects (e.g., videos, songs), and the ability to disseminate them easier than ever. Meanwhile, they were surprised and none too happy to hear that evidence showed that access to information and technological tools did not necessarily mean people were more *creative* in their cultural production. Maybe it was easier for anyone to make cultural products, but were these products more innovative? For instance, research shows that in scholarly work, the wider access to information facilitated by the availability of digital sources has not led to a wider use of information. Quite the contrary, access to electronic information has narrowed the range of articles that get cited, not expanded it (Evans, 2008). Anybody who has read an article from a journal website or search engine can easily understand why this is the case: when we read an article, we are presented with information about not only publications cited in this article but also other publications that cite this article, or articles related to this one. Much like Spotify or similar streaming services, this tends to narrow the limitless range of options to just a few sources that draw our collective attention.

Much as we were confronted with the contrast between students' assumptions and our own, it is instructive to take stock of the normative views that have long informed the understanding of creativity as a phenomenon associated with the lone genius and the romantic image of the artist devoted to art for art's sake. Just as importantly, we would do well to take stock of the deeply ingrained sociological emphasis on the weight of constraints on cognition and action. In this book, we have sought to show that we are better off moving away from either one or the other ends of the spectrum. Likewise, we have sought to show that once we move away from the assumption that creativity and innovation entail exceptional breakthroughs and involve unique figures – whether because we believe the weight of social constraints is such that innovation can only occur in exceptional occasions or because the lone genius required for a breakthrough is statistically rare – we can begin to understand creativity and innovation as more ordinary occurrences. Throughout the book chapters, we have thus looked at the social factors that inform creative work, including those that facilitate novel thinking and the creation of innovative products as well as those that introduce constraints.

At the center of the social study of creativity lies a paradox. As an object of study, creativity lends itself to sociological analysis. Indeed, many, if not most, of the central perspectives in the sociology of culture could well be considered frameworks for the study of creative work, from the agonistic approach originated in Bourdieu's field theoretical apparatus to the collaborative emphasis of Becker's art worlds. At the same time, for all their differences, these perspectives share a focus on the constraining effects of social forces on thinking and action. So where is creativity? If we understand creativity as the departure from established ways of doing things, is this not a breaking away from the constraints imposed by conventions, technical infrastructures, cultural capital, social connections, or status? The path forward in sociological research on creativity ought to find a middle ground between the lay understanding of creativity as freely and easily attainable thanks to technological advancements (dramatically accelerated through investments in artificial intelligence at the moment) and the sociological emphasis on constraints.

With its preoccupation with constraints, sociological research has lagged behind other disciplines in the study of creativity. Indeed, the interest in creativity is still rather marginal in sociology. The psychology of creativity, by contrast, began to develop as a field of study in the 1950s, and has grown to be a large and central field within that discipline. As such, it has contributed enormously to how we understand creativity. But this means that much of the understanding of creativity has revolved around intra-individual processes. Psychologists have looked at a variety of psychological processes to explain individual differences in creativity, including cognition, motivation, affect, emotions, and biology. It took a couple of decades (the 1970s–1980s) until they slowly began to incorporate attention to socio-cultural factors in the analysis of creativity, and we have discussed this important work in the book.

Of course, when sociologists study creativity, they place creative processes within social environments. Creativity is not simply seen as embedded in a social context, but it is rather seen as accomplished through (and, fundamentally, constrained by) the interconnections between individuals, as well as between people and objects, the physical environment, organizations, and institutions. As Todd Lubart et al. (2019: 423) evocatively suggest in a piece on cultural perspectives on creativity, creativity happens "'in between' people and the cultural environment rather than 'inside the head'."

Precisely because there is a rich interdisciplinary body of work on creativity and innovation, we have drawn on many different disciplines and perspectives to offer as broad an approach as possible to the understanding of creativity. We have drawn on varied social sciences that, unlike sociology, have made creativity and innovation a central object of study, especially psychology, anthropology, and organizational studies. We have drawn on interdisciplinary areas such as materiality studies, and social studies of sciences and technology, and have also covered disciplines such as cognitive psychology and cognitive neuroscience, which have been fertile terrains for the study of creativity.

What have we learned? We began this book with an introduction to creativity as a social phenomenon, a history of the conceptualization of creativity, and a brief overview of social theories about creativity. We could not write a book about culture and creativity without beginning with a discussion of the main sociological perspectives on cultural production, so this is what the first chapter covers. In all, the chapters that comprise this book are dedicated to different social dimensions that have been shown to be central in shaping creativity. The chapter on culture provides an overview of a wide range of social and cultural factors, from the role of conventions, laws, and institutions, to norms, social relations, and reputations. The chapter on objects shows how the materials people work with – from the type of paint visual artists use to supplies in a biology lab – inform the kind of ideas and products people may come up with, limiting what is possible in some ways and leading to creative breakthroughs in others. This chapter reviews materiality studies and work in the sociology of culture that shed light on how material objects inform creative work in the arts and sciences, and pays special attention to social studies of science and technology as this perspective has been among the first and most influential in the study of the role of objects in scientific discovery. The following chapter looks at cognition, reviewing information from the cognitive sciences (writ large) on how cognitive processes influence the ways in which creators approach their work and likelihood that they will come up with original ideas, and draws on research in sociology and other social sciences that sheds light on how cognition shapes the creation of ideas and production of cultural objects. The last chapter homes in on social structures, and looks at the ways in which organizations influence people's ability to be innovative and how organizational structures shape patterns of creativity and innovation. In addition, it examines the role of social networks in explaining people's differential access to information and potential for collaboration, as well as the diffusion of novel creations. Lastly, it discusses how the physical attributes of space also inform the degree of innovation we will find in a given area of activity.

All these areas of study may have sometimes seemed like different silos, given how distinct their analytic foci are. The kinds of laboratory studies made famous by Latour and his followers (e.g., Latour, 1988; Latour and Woolgar, 1979), for instance, have little in common with Zuckerman and colleagues' research on organizations (e.g., Phillips and Zuckerman, 2001; Zuckerman, 1999). Some of the literature we covered has a more narrow focus and was therefore only discussed in one chapter (e.g., Latour, 1988), whereas other prominent works speak to more than one area of study, and we highlighted different dimensions of these works across chapters (e.g., Bourdieu, 1990; Collins, 2004). Now that we have discussed each separate dimension, we can take stock of what we have covered and inquire whether the scholarly literature on creativity offers explanations and analyses that – with their disparate foci – are nonetheless complementary, or whether their findings are in tension with one another.

There is probably no better example of works that are pitched against each other but are rather complementary than Becker's (1982) art worlds and Bourdieu's (1993) theory of fields of cultural production. Even in the pages of this book, we have underscored the difference between their approaches, with Becker's focus on collaboration and Bourdieu's on antagonistic competition. Becker (2008) himself, in the epilogue to the 25th anniversary edition of *Art Worlds*, acknowledges that there is more in common between the two theories than it has been made out to be. The two authors, as Becker states, are not in profound disagreement about the nature of creative work, or the extent to which creators are pitted against each other in an agonic struggle for prestige or are embedded in networks of cooperation and collaboration. Rather, Becker and Bourdieu focused on different sets of constraints on creative work, shedding light on what may have appeared to be contradictory forces but may well be complementary. But no other major perspective we covered in this book is pitted against another quite like these two. So the most productive question that lies ahead of us is less about ontological assumptions underpinning theories (are people prone to cooperation or are they embedded in a constant struggle to improve their own social positions?) and more about the overall themes that transpire from the literature on creativity we have reviewed and the lessons we have learned about patterns in creativity.

Levels of Analysis in Creativity

A few themes, or levels of analysis, come through clearly across the chapters in this book, independent of perspectives and disciplines. These themes can be organized as follows: individual creativity, creativity within social environments, creativity among people, and process and outcome in creativity.

Let us start, as the literature on creativity itself began (see Sawyer, 2006; Shapin, 2020a), with the theorization of individual attributes that explain creative patterns. We have learned that, contrary to lay assumptions that associate creativity with particular cognitive patterns (e.g., the individual genius who comes up with new ideas out of the blue, the deliberate thinking patterns of innovators), different cognitive patterns may lead to creativity. Yet, the capacity to make connections across different silos (e.g., groups within an organization, areas of activity, types of objects) is often highlighted as a key source for creative thinking, an idea first introduced by Koestler's (1964) classic book on creativity. Social-psychological attributes have also been identified as important, especially how people's sense of self as creators guides them in their creative choices and careers (Gross, 2008; Leschziner, 2015), as well as how creators assess their thinking processes (Thompson, 2009). To this, we can add the life course perspective on creativity, which identifies different stages in people's creative work and breakthroughs that are explained by creators' age and seniority and the type of work they do (e.g., Galenson, 2006).

To be sure, the main sociological lesson (and one first developed by social psychologists) is that even if creative individuals work independently, they are embedded in social environments that inform their ideas as well as the products they put out in the world. Here, we learned about how people obtain ideas from peers in their small social circles, from how social group dynamics shape creativity patterns (Farrell, 2001) to how social network structures explain where innovation is likely to arise (Collins, 1998). We also learned about how larger social environments shape creative patterns, from Becker's (1982) art worlds perspective, shedding light on how stylistic conventions, support staff, technical and material constraints, and legal and institutional frameworks all constrain what creators can do, to Bourdieu's (1993) field theoretical perspective, with its emphasis on the constraints introduced by people's status positions within a field and the resources (capital) that people have accrued, and how these determine the type of work people are most likely to do.

Beyond these foundational works, there is a vast literature focused on the structural attributes of larger environments and how they influence creativity and innovation patterns. The literature is distinguished between research that investigates the structural attributes of organizational configurations (e.g., Phillips and Zuckerman, 2001; White and White, 1965) and those of social networks (e.g., Burt, 2004; Cattani et al., 2015), and this is indeed how we introduced these bodies of work. Their fundamental difference in focus aside, these two bodies of work have in common the overall insight that people's social location vis-à-vis others working in the same domain of activity – i.e., their status positions in their organizational configurations or their location in a social network – has a large influence on both the type of information people may access and the reception their creations will receive.

A smaller but important body of work combines the investigation of the role of the environment on creativity with a focus on the spatial and material attributes of the space or place (e.g., Benzecry, 2022; Borowiecki, 2013; Molotch, 2003; Oberlin and Gieryn, 2015; Phillips, 2013). While another body of work mostly focuses on the material attributes of the local environment and its affordances and how these shape what people create (e.g., DeNora, 2000; Domínguez Rubio, 2020; Knorr-Cetina, 1999).

But it is one thing to place creators within social environments and investigate how the latter influence creativity patterns, and another to examine how creators produce objects together. Collaborative creativity is another theme in the literature on creativity, though more common in research on innovation in organizations than in the sociological literature, to no small degree because organizations typically have departments dedicated to research and innovation (e.g., R&D departments) where staff are hired to work together, and this is a focus of interest in organizational research (e.g., Elsbach and Flynn, 2013). The sociology of culture literature, however, has more commonly examined individual creativity, as we have seen; though there are a number of exemplars that have focused on collaboration, chief among which is of course Farrell's (2001) work on "collaborative circles" but also the unique research on collective creativity in the South Pacific done by Katherine Giuffre (2009). More recently, there has been a resurgence of cultural sociological work that sheds light on the active process of creating artistic work in groups (e.g., Brett, 2022; De Laat, 2015; Price, 2020). These and a few other exemplars aside, even sociological research that examines work in science typically focuses on individual attributes more than collective collaboration (e.g., Duede et al., 2024), even though collaboration has become increasingly common, including in disciplines where individual production used to be the norm (e.g., sociology). Thus, while collaboration is an important theme in creative work, it is one that merits more sociological attention than it has received.

If collaboration highlights what creators achieve together, an equally pressing question is how to account for the role of the individual within these collective processes. This last point remains one of the key unexplored topics in sociological accounts of culture and creativity: what role does individual talent play (Menger, 2018), even when treated as embedded in social and material relationships? The literatures on networks, social studies of science and technology, field theory, interaction ritual chains, art worlds, and the production of culture all converge on seeing the individual within a configuration of relationships, leading us to ask about the symmetry (or asymmetry) among actors. We have become adept at showing how genius is socially produced, but as sociologists often invested in debunking creativity as myth – made from collaboration and the division of labor – we lag in explaining what, from those individuals (such as Mozart, Beethoven, Manet, Rodin, Hawking, Pasteur, García Márquez, to name some of the canonical figures mentioned in this book), contributed to the innovative character of their work. One of the most striking questions raised by Mialet's (2012) research on Hawking is whether anyone in his network of collaborators could have replaced him in the production of theoretical physics work of equal innovation, or whether there is something singular in his contribution that we still need to make sense of.

The last theme we mentioned above is creative process and outcome. This is a theme that cuts across all the other ones, residing at a different level of analysis. The question of what influences the creative process, as well as what the process of creation might look like, is indeed an important theme across all research on creativity. This is a distinct area of inquiry from the question of what social factors determine the outcome of the creative process, a question that includes how and whether an idea effectively becomes a finished product, as well as how a finished product will fare among audiences (peers or the larger public). These two areas of inquiry have led to the scholarly divide between creativity and innovation, where the former is associated with the process of creation and the latter with the outcome of such a process.

A fairly consensual distinction posits that creativity is about the process whereby people come up with novel ideas, whereas innovation is only defined as such if, and only if, there is a material outcome of the creative process (e.g., an object, resource, or technique) and the outcome is socially regarded as an innovation with valuable implications (see for instance Opazo, 2016: 12). It is worthy of note that most research investigates either the process or the outcome of creativity. This is understandable given the scope of the undertaking, but it does mean that we have limited knowledge on whether and how the two may be related. Childress' (2017) research on the whole cycle of creative production in the book industry is a rare exception, as it follows the life of a book from the ideation to the reception of the cultural product. Focusing on the life of one book, this project does not aim to identify patterns of creativity, let alone whether patterns in the creative process have any association with the outcomes of the process. So this remains an unexplored question, and one that could lead to productive new research that could go in many different directions, examining the different topics we covered across the chapters and some of the themes we highlighted in these last pages.

Lessons for the Study of Creativity

From the themes above, a few common lessons arise for those interested in studying creativity. Our goal is not to wield a corrosive sociological skepticism that dissolves the "myth" of creativity until the only conclusion is that innovation does not exist; rather, it is to take claims about creativity seriously and examine them in their own terms, step by step. Since there is no meta perspective in the sociological study of creativity, what emerges is closer to a cubist approach, through which each theme and research strategy partially illuminates the object, highlighting certain dimensions while leaving others in the background.

The first lesson that emerges from what we already know about creativity is to always look for the support structures that make a breakthrough possible. Rarely do innovations emerge in isolation; they are embedded in webs of backing, collaboration, and logistical scaffolding. One must ask: what institutions or agencies provided the funding? Which colleagues contributed ideas, resources, or expertise? Who were the technicians, assistants, or support staff whose work, often invisible, enabled the result to take shape? To understand a discovery fully is to trace these infrastructures of possibility, rather than focusing only on the individual credited with the achievement.

The second lesson is to situate the individual or group responsible for a breakthrough within the broader field of relations that both constrain and enable their success. Breakthroughs are never solely about the ingenuity of one actor but about their position relative to others – competitors pushing in similar directions, distributors who give visibility to their work, collaborators who share knowledge and resources, and evaluators and gatekeepers who determine legitimacy. Who recognized and consecrated the achievement? How did their endorsement – or lack thereof – shape the trajectory of the innovation? At stake are not only the intrinsic merits of the creation but also the shifting dynamics of reputation, status, and influence: those who began at the margins may, by the end, find themselves at the center of the field. Or not. But whether they end up at the center or not is not simply based on their talent, but also on all the social, organizational, and material infrastructure that shapes what is possible and how those possibilities will be received by peers and audiences.

The third lesson is to examine the product itself and reconstruct the process that led to its completion. This means paying attention to the materials mobilized, the exchange of ideas, the sequence of steps taken to produce the object, and the affordances and constraints that established ideas, materials, and collaborators and support staff introduced. It also requires asking how and when a work comes to be recognized as finished, since closure is rarely self-evident but the outcome of conventions, negotiations, and institutional practices. Of course, such an approach carries its own challenges: the retrospective narratives that chart a path to success impose a teleology, privileging the completed and consecrated over the unfinished or forgotten. Yet even with these limits, historical reconstruction remains a powerful strategy for analyzing how creativity unfolds, showing not only the variations in process but also the ways in which materiality itself participates in shaping the outcome.

The fourth lesson, related but distinct from the previous one, is to enter the study of creativity not through its triumphs, but through its fractures – failure, breakdown, and conflict. Creativity is not only forged in moments of inspiration, but equally, and perhaps more revealingly, in episodes where the act of creation falters or collapses. What structural, organizational, or interpersonal conditions precipitated the breakdown of a project? Why did an initiative fail to yield novel outcomes, even when it shared material resources, personnel, and institutional support with other, more successful endeavors? These moments of collapse are analytically generative: they unearth the often-invisible scaffolding that supports creative work – shared assumptions, tacit norms, and interdependencies – by making visible what happens when those elements unravel. Moreover, attending to conflict forces us to foreground the social actors involved: who advocated for competing visions of the project, and on what grounds? What forms of authority or legitimacy were invoked in these disputes? Conflict brings into relief the interpretive and political work of creativity – the labor of framing a contribution as original, of enrolling others into a new paradigm, and of resisting or negotiating dominant standards. In this view, failure and disagreement are not peripheral to creativity; they are central arenas in which the very meaning of innovation is contested and forged.

The fifth lesson – and one of the most conceptually complex in the study of creativity – is to assess the role of the individual within fundamentally collaborative settings. While it is now widely accepted that creative work is rarely, if ever, the product of a single mind, this recognition should not obscure the possibility that collaborations are often asymmetrical by design or necessity. Not all contributors occupy the same position in relation to the core intellectual, aesthetic, or technical direction of a project. Some individuals bring singular expertise, cultivated craft, or visionary capacity that decisively shapes the outcome in ways others could not have replicated. This does not diminish the importance of support roles or collective effort, but it raises a critical question: in what cases does a particular individual make a contribution so specific, so tied to their unique formation, that it becomes irreplaceable? And how do we analytically identify such contributions without reverting to myths of isolated genius? Attending to these distinctions allows us to better understand the internal structure of collaboration – how different forms of knowledge, skill, and authorship come together, sometimes unevenly, to produce creative work. Rather than treating collaboration and individuality as opposing forces, this perspective invites us to examine how they are dynamically configured in practice.

Culture and Creativity promised in its introduction to put creativity and innovation through a semantic therapy, helping to stabilize the definition of the phenomenon, identifying the different theories under which creativity and innovation have been defined and studied. To do this, we identified key cases to take lessons from, and some core themes across multiple literatures, generating a modest proposal for best practices for how to investigate creativity as a sociological problem. While the book is not intended to resolve disjunctures in what often appear as scattered perspectives on creativity, we hope it can help readers move closer to a more comprehensive understanding of how creativity happens, and guide them in making sense of this elusive and complex phenomenon.

Notes

1 Contrary to this argument, David Galenson and Robert Jensen (2007) suggest that the actions of a few key artists were the driving force behind the demise of the Salon. Dealers, according to these authors, did not begin to show and support the work of untried contemporary artists (i.e., those who had not yet acquired high reputation in group shows) until the twentieth century.

2 Bourdieu has also written about fields of restricted production and fields of large-scale production as two independent fields.

References

Alexander, V. (2018) "Heteronomy in the Arts Field: State Funding and British Arts Organizations," *British Journal of Sociology*, 69(1), pp. 23–43.

Allen, A.P. and Thomas, K.E. (2011) "A Dual Process Account of Creative Thinking," *Creativity Research Journal*, 23(2), pp. 109–18.

Amabile, T.M. and Pillemer, J. (2012) "Perspectives on the Social Psychology of Creativity," *Journal of Creative Behavior*, 46(1), pp. 3–15.

Anand, N. and Peterson, R.A. (2000) "When Market Information Constitutes Fields: Sensemaking of Markets in the Commercial Music Industry," *Organization Science*, 11(3), pp. 270–84.

Atkinson, P. (2006) *Everyday Arias: An Operatic Ethnography*. Lanham, MD: AltaMira Press.

Audretsch, D.B. and Feldman, M.P. (1996) "R&D Spillovers and the Geography of Innovation and Production," *The American Economic Review*, 86(3), pp. 630–40.

Bago, B. and De Neys, W. (2020) "Advancing the Specification of Dual Process Models of Higher Cognition: A Critical Test of the Hybrid Model View," *Thinking & Reasoning*, 26(1), pp. 1–30.

Barbalet, J. (2011) "Emotions Beyond Regulation: Backgrounded Emotions in Science and Trust," *Emotion Review*, 3(1), pp. 36–43.

Bargh, J.A., Schwader, K.L., Hailey, S.E., Dyer, R.L., and Boothby, E.J. (2012) "Automaticity in Social-Cognitive Processes," *Trends in Cognitive Sciences*, 16(12), pp. 593–605.

Barker III, V.L. and Mueller, G.C. (2002) "CEO Characteristics and Firm R&D Spending," *Management Science*, 48(6), pp. 782–801.

Barsalou, L.W. (1999) "Perceptual Symbol Systems," *Behavioral and Brain Sciences*, 22(4), pp. 577–660.

Barthes, R. (1972) "The Brain of Einstein," in *Mythologies*. New York: Farrar, Straus and Giroux.

References

Baumann, S. (2007) *Hollywood Highbrow: From Entertainment to Art.* Princeton, NJ: Princeton University Press.

Becker, H.S. (1995) "The Power of Inertia," *Sociological Forum*, 1(1), pp. 1–18.

Becker, H.S. ([1982] 2008) *Art Worlds.* Oakland: University of California Press.

Becker, H.S. and Faulkner, R.R. (2009) *Do You Know...? The Jazz Repertoire in Action.* Chicago: University of Chicago Press.

Becker, H.S. and Faulkner, R.R. (2013) *Thinking Together: An Email Exchange and All That Jazz.* Chicago: University of Chicago Press.

Becker, H.S., Faulkner, R.R., and Kirshenblatt-Gimblett, B. (eds.) (2006) *Art from Start to Finish: Jazz, Painting, Writing, and Other Improvisations.* Chicago: University of Chicago Press.

Becker, M.C., Lazaric, N., Nelson, R.R., and Winter, S.G. (2005) "Applying Organizational Routines in Understanding Organizational Change," *Industrial and Corporate Change*, 14(5), pp. 775–91.

Benzecry, C.E. (2006) "Curtain Rising, Baton Falling: The Politics of Musical Conducting in Contemporary Argentina," *Theory and Society*, 35(4), pp. 445–79.

Benzecry, C.E. (2022) *The Perfect Fit: Creative Work in the Global Shoe Industry.* Chicago: University of Chicago Press.

Benzecry, C.E. and Domínguez Rubio, F. (2018) "The Cultural Life of Objects," in Grindstaff, L., Lo, M.-C.M., and Hall, J.R. (eds.) *Routledge Handbook of Cultural Sociology.* Abingdon: Routledge, pp. 322–9.

Bishop, S. (2025) "Influencer Creep: How Artists Strategically Navigate the Platformisation of Art Worlds," *New Media & Society*, 27(4), pp. 2109–26.

Blair, H. (2001) "'You're Only as Good as Your Last Job': The Labour Process and Labour Market in the British Film Industry," *Work, Employment and Society*, 15(1), pp. 149–69.

Boczkowski, P.J. (2010) *News at Work: Imitation in an Age of Information Abundance.* Chicago: University of Chicago Press.

Borowiecki, K.J. (2013) "Geographic Clustering and Productivity: An Instrumental Variable Approach for Classical Composers," *Journal of Urban Economics*, 73(1), pp. 94–110.

Bottero, W. and Crossley, N. (2011) "Worlds, Fields and Networks: Becker, Bourdieu, and the Structures of Social Relations," *Cultural Sociology*, 5(1), pp. 99–119.

Bourdieu, P. (1984) *Distinction: A Social Critique of the Judgment of Taste.* Cambridge, MA: Harvard University Press.

Bourdieu, P. (1986) "The Forms of Capital," in Richardson, J.G. (ed.) *Handbook of Theory and Research for the Sociology of Education.* New York: Greenwood Press, pp. 241–58.

Bourdieu, P. (1988) *Homo Academicus.* Cambridge: Polity Press.

References

Bourdieu, P. ([1980] 1990) *The Logic of Practice*. Stanford, CA: Stanford University Press.

Bourdieu, P. (1992) *The Rules of Art: Genesis and Structure of the Literary Field*. Stanford, CA: Stanford University Press.

Bourdieu, P. (1993) *The Field of Cultural Production*. New York: Columbia University Press.

Bourdieu, P. (2017) *Manet: A Symbolic Revolution*. London: Polity Press.

Bowker, G.C. and Star, S.L. (1999) *Sorting Things Out: Classification and its Consequences*. Cambridge, MA: MIT Press.

Brett, G. (2022) "Dueling with Dual-Process Models: Cognition, Creativity, and Context," *Sociological Theory*, 40(2), pp. 179–201.

Burt, R.S. (2004) "Structural Holes and Good Ideas," *American Journal of Sociology*, 110(2), pp. 349–99.

Callon, M. (1986) "Some Elements of a Sociology of Translation: Domestication of the Scallops and the Fishermen of St. Brieuc Bay," in Law, J. (ed.) *Power, Action and Belief: A New Sociology of Knowledge?* London: Routledge, pp. 196–233.

Camic, C. (1986) "The Matter of Habit," *American Journal of Sociology*, 91(5), pp. 1039–87.

Camic, C. and Gross, N. (2004) "The New Sociology of Ideas," in Blau, J.R. (ed.) *Blackwell Companion to Sociology*. Oxford: Blackwell, pp. 236–49.

Cao, L., Chen, Z., and Evans, J.A. (2022) "Destructive Creation, Creative Destruction, and the Paradox of Innovation Science," *Sociology Compass*, 16(11), e13043.

Cattani, G., Ferriani, S., and Allison, P.D. (2014) "Insiders, Outsiders, and the Struggle for Consecration in Cultural Fields: A Core–Periphery Perspective," *American Sociological Review*, 79(2), pp. 258–81.

Cattani, G., Ferriani, S., and Colucci, M. (2015) "Creativity in Social Networks: A Core–Periphery Perspective," in Jones, C., Lorenzen, M., and Sapsed, J. (eds.) *The Oxford Handbook of Creative Industries*. Oxford: Oxford University Press, pp. 75–95.

Cerulo, K.A. (2018) *Embodiment and the Sociology of Meaning*. Cambridge: Polity Press.

Childress, C. (2017) *Under the Cover: The Creation, Production, and Reception of a Novel*. Princeton, NJ: Princeton University Press.

Childress, C. and Gerber, A. (2015) "The MFA in Creative Writing: The Uses of a 'Useless' Credential," *Professions and Professionalism*, 5(2), pp. 1–16.

Childress, C., Rawlings, C.M., and Moeran, B. (2017) "Publishers, Authors, and Texts: The Process of Cultural Consecration in Prize Evaluation," *Poetics*, 60, pp. 48–61.

Chong, P. (2019) *Inside the Critics' Circle: Book Reviewing in Uncertain Times*. Princeton, NJ: Princeton University Press.

Christin, A. (2020) *Metrics at Work: Journalism and the Contested Meaning of Algorithms*. Princeton, NJ: Princeton University Press.
Clark, A. (1997) *Being There: Putting Brain, Body, and World Together Again*. Cambridge, MA: MIT Press.
Clark, A. (1999) "An Embodied Cognitive Science?," *Trends in Cognitive Sciences*, 3(9), pp. 345–51.
Clark, A. and Chalmers, D. (1998) "The Extended Mind," *Analysis*, 58(1), pp. 7–19.
Collins, R. (1998) *The Sociology of Philosophies: A Global Theory of Intellectual Change*. Cambridge, MA: Harvard University Press.
Collins, R. (2004) *Interaction Ritual Chains*. Princeton, NJ: Princeton University Press.
Corte, U. (2013) "A Refinement of Collaborative Circles Theory: Resource Mobilization and Innovation in an Emerging Sport," *Social Psychology Quarterly*, 76(1), pp. 25–51.
Craig, A. (2007) "Practicing Poetry: A Career Without a Job," in Calhoun, C. and Sennett, R. (eds.) *Practicing Culture*. New York: Routledge, pp. 147–65.
Craig, A. and Dubois, S. (2010) "Between Art and Money: The Social Space of Public Readings in Contemporary Poetry Economies and Careers," *Poetics*, 38(5), pp. 441–60.
Crane, D. (1987) *The Transformation of the Avant-Garde: The New York Art World, 1940–1985*. Chicago: University of Chicago Press.
Csikszentmihalyi, M. (1996) *Creativity: Flow and the Psychology of Discovery and Invention*. New York: HarperCollins.
Currid-Halkett, E. (2009) *The Warhol Economy: How Fashion, Art, and Music Drive New York City*. Oxford: Princeton University Press.
Dalton, B. (2004) "Creativity, Habit, and the Social Products of Creative Action: Revising Joas, Incorporating Bourdieu," *Sociological Theory* 22(4), pp. 603–22.
Davis, G.A. (1999) "Barriers to Creativity and Creative Attitudes," in Runco, M.A. and Pritzker, S.R. (eds.) *Encyclopedia of Creativity*. San Diego, CA: Academic Press, pp. 165–74.
Davis, J.L. and Chouinard, J.B. (2016) "Theorizing Affordances: From Request to Refuse," *Bulletin of Science, Technology & Society*, 36(4), pp. 241–8.
de Courson, B., Thouzeau, V., and Baumard, N. (2023) "Quantifying the Scientific Revolution," *Evolutionary Human Sciences*, 5(e19), pp. 1–22.
De Laat, K. (2015) "Write a Word, Get a Third: Managing Conflict and Rewards in Professional Songwriting Teams," *Work and Occupations*, 42(2), pp. 225–56.
DeNora, T. (1991) "Musical Patronage and Social Change in Beethoven's Vienna," *American Journal of Sociology*, 97(2), pp. 310–46.
DeNora, T. (1997) "Beethoven and the Construction of Genius: Musical Politics in Vienna, 1792–1803," *The Musical Quarterly*, 80(1), pp. 1–30.

DeNora, T. (2000) *Music in Everyday Life*. Cambridge: Cambridge University Press.
DeNora, T. (2002) "Music as a Technology of the Self," *Poetics*, 27(1), pp. 31–56.
Dewey, J. ([1922] 2002) *Human Nature and Conduct: An Introduction to Social Psychology*. New York: Dover Publications.
DiMaggio, P. (1982) "Cultural Entrepreneurship in Nineteenth-Century Boston: The Creation of an Organizational Base for High Culture in America," *Media, Culture & Society*, 4(1), pp. 33–50.
DiMaggio, P.J. and Powell, W.W. (1983) "The Iron Cage Revisited: Institutional Isomorphism and Collective Rationality in Organizational Fields," *American Sociological Review*, 48(2), pp. 147–60.
Domínguez Rubio, F. (2020) *Still Life: Ecologies of the Modern Imagination at the Art Museum*. Chicago: University of Chicago Press.
Domínguez Rubio, F. and Silva, E.B. (2014) "Materials in the Field: Object-Trajectories and Object-Positions in the Field of Contemporary Art," *Cultural Sociology*, 7(2), pp. 161–78.
Dowd, T.J., Liddle, K., and Borden, A. (2002) "Organizing the Musical Canon: The Repertoires of Major U.S. Symphony Orchestras, 1842 to 1969," *Poetics*, 30(1–2), pp. 35–61.
Duede, E., Teplitskiy, M., Lakhani, K., and Evans, J. (2024) "Being Together in Place as a Catalyst for Scientific Advance," *Research Policy*, 53, 104911.
Duffy, B.E. (2017) *(Not) Getting Paid to Do What You Love: Gender, Social Media, and Aspirational Work*. New Haven, CT and London: Yale University Press.
Elsbach, K.D. and Flynn, F.J. (2013) "Creative Collaboration and the Self-Concept: A Study of Toy Designers," *Journal of Management Studies*, 50(4), pp. 515–44.
Evans, J.E. (2008) "Electronic Publication and the Narrowing of Science and Scholarship," *Science*, 321, pp. 395–9.
Evans, J. St. B.T. and Stanovich, K.E. (2013) "Dual-Process Theories of Higher Cognition: Advancing the Debate: Advancing the Debate," *Perspectives on Psychological Science*, 8(3), pp. 223–41.
Fang, J. (2025) "The Culture of Censorship: State Intervention and Complicit Creativity in Global Film Production," *American Sociological Review*, 89, pp. 488–517.
Farrell, M.P. (2001) *Collaborative Circles: Friendship Dynamics and Creative Work*. Chicago: University of Chicago Press.
Faulkner, R.R. ([1983] 1987) *Music on Demand: Composers and Careers in the Hollywood Film Industry*. New Brunswick, NJ: Transaction Publishers.
Ferrary, M. and Granovetter, M. (2009) "The Role of Venture Capital Firms in Silicon Valley's Complex Innovation Network," *Economy and Society*, 38(2), pp. 326–59.

Fine, G.A. (2003) "Crafting Authenticity: The Validation of Identity in Self-Taught Art," *Theory and Society*, 32(2), pp. 153–80.
Fine, G.A. (2004) *Everyday Genius: Self-Taught Art and the Culture of Authenticity*. Chicago: University of Chicago Press.
Fligstein, N. (2021) "Innovation and the Theory of Fields," *AMS Review*, 11(3), pp. 272–89.
Fligstein, N. and McAdam, D. (2011) "Toward a General Theory of Strategic Action Fields," *Sociological Theory*, 29(1), pp. 1–26.
Fligstein, N. and McAdam, D. (2012) *A Theory of Fields*. New York: Oxford University Press.
Florida, R. (2002) *The Rise of the Creative Class: And How it's Transforming Work, Leisure, Community, and Everyday Life*. New York: Basic Books.
Florida, R. (2005) *Cities and the Creative Class*. New York: Routledge.
Franklin, S. (2023) *The Origins of Creativity's Explosion in the U.S.* Chicago: University of Chicago Press.
Franks, D.D. (2014) "Emotions as Organizing and Moving the Brain," in Stets, J.E. and Turner, J.H. (eds.) *Handbook of the Sociology of Emotions: Volume II*. Dordrecht: Springer, pp. 267–81.
Frenette, A. (2013) "Making the Intern Economy: Role and Career Challenges of the Music Industry Intern," *Work and Occupations*, 40(4), pp. 364–97.
Frenette, A. (2019) "Leveraging Youth: Overcoming Intergenerational Tensions in Creative Production," *Social Psychology Quarterly*, 82(4), pp. 386–406.
Frenette, A. (2026) *Blame the Intern: On (Not) Breaking into the Creative Economy*. Princeton, NJ: Princeton University Press.
Frickel, S. (2004) *Chemical Consequences: Environmental Mutagens, Scientist Activism, and the Rise of Genetic Toxicology*. New Brunswick, NJ: Rutgers University Press.
Gabora, L. and Ranjan, A. (2013) "How Insight Emerges in Distributed, Content-Addressable Memory," in Vartanian, O., Bristol, A.S., and Kaufman, J.C. (eds.) *Neuroscience of Creativity*. Cambridge, MA: MIT Press, pp. 19–44.
Galenson, D.W. (2006) *Old Masters and Young Geniuses: The Two Life Cycles of Artistic Creativity*. Princeton, NJ: Princeton University Press.
Galenson, D.W. and Jensen, R. (2007) "Careers and Canvases: The Rise of the Market for Modern Art in Nineteenth-Century Paris," in Stolwijk, C. (ed.) *Current Issues in 19th-Century Art: Van Gogh Studies 1*. Zwolle: Van Gogh Museum, Amsterdam: Waanders Publishers, pp. 137–66.
Galison, P. (2003) *Einstein's Clocks, Poincaré's Maps: Empires of Time*. New York: W.W. Norton.
Gardner, H. (1993) *Creating Minds: An Anatomy of Creativity Seen Through the Lives of Freud, Einstein, Picasso, Stravinsky, Eliot, Graham, and Gandhi*. New York: Basic Books.
Gibson, J.J. (1979) *The Ecological Approach to Visual Perception*. Boston: Houghton Mifflin.

Gieryn, T.F. (2006) "City as Truth-Spot: Laboratories and Field Sites in Urban Studies," *Social Studies of Science*, 36(1), pp. 5–38.
Gillespie, T. (2014) "The Relevance of Algorithms," in Gillespie, T., Boczkowski, P., and Foot, K. (eds.) *Media Technologies: Essays on Communication, Materiality, and Society*. Cambridge, MA: MIT Press, pp. 167–94.
Gillespie, T. (2018) *Custodians of the Internet: Platforms, Content Moderation, and the Hidden Decisions That Shape Social Media*. New Haven, CT: Yale University Press.
Giuffre, K. (2009) *Collective Creativity: Art and Society in the South Pacific*. Farnham, UK; Burlington, VT: Ashgate.
Gladwell, M. (2002) *The Tipping Point: How Little Things Can Make a Big Difference*. Boston: Little, Brown and Company.
Glăveanu, V.P. (2012) "Habitual Creativity: Revising Habit, Reconceptualizing Creativity," *Review of General Psychology*, 16(1), pp. 78–92.
Glăveanu, V.P. (2014) *Distributed Creativity: Thinking Outside the Box of the Creative Individual*. Cham: Springer International Publishing.
Godart, F.C. and Mears, A. (2009) "How Do Cultural Producers Make Creative Decisions? Lessons from the Catwalk," *Social Forces*, 88(2), pp. 671–92.
Godart, F.C., Shipilov, A.V., and Claes, K. (2014) "Making the Most of the Revolving Door: The Impact of Outward Personnel Mobility Networks on Organizational Creativity," *Organization Science*, 25(2), pp. 377–400.
Godart, F., Seong, S., and Phillips, D.J. (2020) "The Sociology of Creativity: Elements, Structures, and Audiences," *Annual Review of Sociology*, 46, pp. 489–510.
Granovetter, M. (1973) "The Strength of Weak Ties," *American Journal of Sociology*, 78(6), pp. 1360–80.
Granovetter, M. (1974) *Getting a Job: A Study of Contacts and Careers*. Cambridge, MA: Harvard University Press.
Granovetter, M. (1983) "The Strength of Weak Ties: A Network Theory Revisited," *Sociological Theory*, 1, pp. 201–33.
Griswold, W. (1994) *Cultures and Societies in a Changing World*. New York: Sage.
Griswold, W., Mangione, G., and McDonnell, T.E. (2013) "Objects, Words, and Bodies in Space: Bringing Materiality into Cultural Analysis," *Qualitative Sociology*, 36(4), pp. 343–64.
Gross, N. (2003) "Richard Rorty's Pragmatism: A Case Study in the Sociology of Ideas," *Theory and Society*, 32(1), pp. 93–148.
Gross, N. (2008) *Richard Rorty: The Making of an American Philosopher*. Chicago: University of Chicago Press.
Guetzkow, J., Lamont, M., and Mallard, G. (2004) "What is Originality in the Humanities and the Social Sciences?," *American Sociological Review*, 69(2), pp. 190–212.

Haidt, J. (2021) "The Emotional Dog and its Rational Tail: A Social Intuitionist Approach to Moral Judgment," *Psychological Review*, 108(4), pp. 814–34.
Hannan, M.T. and Freeman, J. (1984) "Structural Inertia and Organizational Change," *American Sociological Review*, 49(2), pp. 149–64.
Hannan, M.T., Pólos, L., and Carroll, G.R. (2004) "The Evolution of Inertia," *Industrial and Corporate Change*, 13(1), pp. 213–42.
Hellmanzik, C. (2010) "Location Matters: Estimating Cluster Premiums for Prominent Modern Artists," *European Economic Review*, 54(2), pp. 199–218.
Hellmanzik, C. (2014) "Prominent Modern Artists: Determinants of Creativity," in Simonton, D.K. (ed.) *The Wiley Handbook of Genius*. Chichester; Malden, MA: Wiley Blackwell, pp. 564–85.
Hennion, A. (1999) "Baroque and Rock: Music, Mediators and Musical Taste," *Poetics*, 26(4), pp. 389–406.
Hennion, A. (2001) "Music Lovers: Taste as Performance," *Theory, Culture & Society*, 18(5), pp. 1–22.
Hennion, A. and Latour, B. (1993) "Objet d'Art, Objet de Science. Note sur les Limites de l'Antifétichisme," *Sociologie de l'Art*, 6, pp. 7–24.
Hesmondhalgh, D. and Baker, S. (2009) "'A Very Complicated Version of Freedom': Conditions and Experiences of Creative Labour in Three Cultural Industries," *Poetics*, 38(1), pp. 4–20.
Hirsch, P.M. (1972) "Processing Fads and Fashions: An Organization-Set Analysis of Cultural Industry Systems," *American Journal of Sociology*, 77(4), pp. 639–59.
Hollingsworth, J.R. (2000) "The Style and Mode of Research Organizations: Innovation in Science," Keynote Address to the Board of Trustees and Members of the Corporation, Neurosciences Research Foundation, La Jolla, CA.
Hutchins, E. (1995) *Cognition in the Wild*. Cambridge, MA: MIT Press.
Ibáñez de Aldecoa, P., de Wit, S., and Tebbich, S. (2021) "Can Habits Impede Creativity by Inducing Fixation?," *Frontiers in Psychology*, 12, 683024.
Ignatow, G. (2007) "Theories of Embodied Knowledge: New Directions for Cultural and Cognitive Sociology?," *Journal for the Theory of Social Behaviour*, 37(2), pp. 115–35.
Jackson, S.J. (2014) "Rethinking Repair," in Gillespie, T., Boczkowski, P.J., and Foot, K. (eds.) *Media Technologies: Essays on Communication, Materiality, and Society*. Cambridge, MA: MIT Press, pp. 221–40.
Jacobs, J. (1969) *The Economy of Cities*. New York: Random House.
Joas, H. (1996) *The Creativity of Action*. Chicago: University of Chicago Press.
Johnson, E.E. (2012) "Intellectual Property and the Incentive Fallacy," *Florida State University Law Review*, 39(3), pp. 623–80.
Keane, W. (2003) "Semiotics and the Social Analysis of Material Things," *Language & Communication*, 23(3–4), pp. 409–25.

Kelly, E. and O'Hagan, J. (2007) "Geographic Clustering of Economic Activity: The Case of Prominent Western Visual Artists," *Journal of Cultural Economics*, 31(2), pp. 109–28.

Kemper, T.D. (1978) *A Social Interactional Theory of Emotions*. New York: Wiley.

Knorr-Cetina, K. (1981) *The Manufacture of Knowledge: An Essay on the Constructivist and Contextual Nature of Science*. Oxford: Pergamon Press.

Knorr-Cetina, K. (1999) *Epistemic Cultures: How the Sciences Make Knowledge*. Cambridge, MA: Harvard University Press.

Koestler, A. (1964) *The Act of Creation*. New York: Macmillan.

Lane, C. and Opazo, M.P. (2024) *Cultural Flows in High-End Cuisine: From the Periphery to the Center*. New York; Abingdon: Routledge.

Latour, B. (1987) *Science in Action: How to Follow Scientists and Engineers through Society*. Cambridge, MA: Harvard University Press.

Latour, B. (1988) *The Pasteurization of France*. Cambridge, MA: Harvard University Press.

Latour, B. (2005) *Reassembling the Social: An Introduction to Actor-Network-Theory*. Oxford: Oxford University Press.

Latour, B. and Woolgar, S. (1979) *Laboratory Life: The Construction of Scientific Facts*. Beverly Hills, CA: Sage.

Lave, J. (1988) *Cognition in Practice: Mind, Mathematics and Culture in Everyday Life*. Cambridge: Cambridge University Press.

Lena, J.C. (2012) *Banding Together: How Communities Create Genres in Popular Music*. Princeton, NJ: Princeton University Press.

Leschziner, V. (2015) *At the Chef's Table: Culinary Creativity in Elite Restaurants*. Stanford, CA: Stanford University Press.

Leschziner, V. and Brett, G. (2019) "Beyond the Individual-Institutional Divide: The Microsociology of Institutional Work," *Theory and Society*, 48(3), pp. 341–66.

Lopes, P.D. (2002) *The Rise of a Jazz Art World*. Cambridge: Cambridge University Press.

Lubart, T., Glăveanu, V.P., de Vries, H., Camargo, A., and Storme, M. (2019) "Cultural Perspectives on Creativity," in Kaufman, J.C. and Sternberg, R.J. (eds.) *The Cambridge Handbook of Creativity*, 2nd edn. Cambridge: Cambridge University Press, pp. 421–47.

Lynch, M. (1985) *Art and Artifact in Laboratory Science: A Study of Shop Work and Shop Talk in a Research Laboratory*. London: Routledge & Kegan Paul.

Mannheim, K. (1936) *Ideology and Utopia: An Introduction to the Sociology of Knowledge*. London: Routledge.

Mannheim, K. (1952) "The Problem of Generations," in Kecskemeti, P. (ed.) *Essays on the Sociology of Knowledge*. London: Routledge, pp. 276–322.

March, J.G. (1991) "Exploration and Exploitation in Organizational Learning," *Organization Science*, 2(1), pp. 71–87.

Mauss, M. ([1934] 1973) "Techniques of the Body," *Economy and Society*, 2(1), pp. 70–88.

McDonnell, T.E. (2016) *Best Laid Plans: Cultural Entropy and the Unraveling of AIDS Media Campaigns*. Chicago: University of Chicago Press.

McDonnell, T.E. (2023) "Cultural Objects, Material Culture, and Materiality," *Annual Review of Sociology*, 49, pp. 195–220.

McLaughlin, N. (2001) "Optimal Marginality: Innovation and Orthodoxy in Fromm's Revision of Psychoanalysis," *The Sociological Quarterly*, 42(2), pp. 271–88.

McLean, P. (2016) *Culture in Networks*. Cambridge; Malden, MA: Polity Press.

Mears, A. (2011) *Pricing Beauty: The Making of a Fashion Model*. Berkeley: University of California Press.

Menger, P.-M. (1999) "Artistic Labor Markets and Careers," *Annual Review of Sociology*, 25, pp. 541–74.

Menger, P.-M. (2001) "Artists as Workers: Theoretical and Methodological Challenges," *Poetics*, 28(4), pp. 241–54.

Menger, P.-M. (2006) "Profiles of the Unfinished: Rodin's Work and the Varieties of Incompleteness," in Becker, H.S., Faulkner, R.R., and Kirshenblatt-Gimblett, B. (eds.) *Art from Start to Finish*. Chicago: University of Chicago Press, pp. 237–78.

Menger, P.-M. (2014) *The Economics of Creativity: Art and Achievement Under Uncertainty*. Cambridge, MA: Harvard University Press.

Menger, P.-M. (ed.) (2018) *Le Talent en Débat*. Paris: PUF.

Merton, R.K. (1957) "Priorities in Scientific Discovery: A Chapter in the Sociology of Science," *American Sociological Review*, 22(6), pp. 635–59.

Merton, R.K. (1968) *Social Theory and Social Structure*. New York: Free Press.

Meyer, J.W. and Rowan, B. (1977) "Institutionalized Organizations: Formal Structure as Myth and Ceremony," *American Journal of Sociology*, 83(2), pp. 340–63.

Mialet, H. (2012) *Hawking Incorporated: Stephen Hawking and the Anthropology of the Knowing Subject*. Chicago: University of Chicago Press.

Miettinen, R. (2006) "The Sources of Novelty: A Cultural and Systemic View of Distributed Creativity," *Creativity and Innovation Management*, 15(2), pp. 173–81.

Moeran, B. (2014) *The Business of Creativity: Toward an Anthropology of Worth*. Walnut Creek, CA: Left Coast Press.

Molotch, H. (2003) *Where Stuff Comes From: How Toasters, Toilets, Cars, Computers, and Many Other Things Come to Be as They Are*. New York: Routledge.

Mould, O. (2019) *Against Creativity*. London: Verso.

Mukerji, C. (2009) *Impossible Engineering: Technology and Territoriality on the Canal du Midi*. Princeton, NJ: Princeton University Press.

Neff, G., Wissinger, E., and Zukin, S. (2005) "Entrepreneurial Labor among

Cultural Producers: 'Cool' Jobs in 'Hot' Industries," *Social Semiotics*, 15(3), pp. 307–34.

Nijstad, B.A., De Dreu, C.K., Rietzschel, E.F., and Baas, M. (2010) "The Dual Pathway to Creativity Model: Creative Ideation as a Function of Flexibility and Persistence," *European Review of Social Psychology*, 21(1), pp. 34–77.

Norman, D.A. (1988) *The Design of Everyday Things*. New York: Doubleday.

Oberlin, K.C. and Gieryn, T.F. (2015) "Place and Culture-Making: Geographic Clumping in the Emergence of Artistic Schools," *Poetics*, 50, pp. 20–43.

Obstfeld, D. (2005) "Social Networks, the Tertius Iungens Orientation, and Involvement in Innovation," *Administrative Science Quarterly*, 50(1), pp. 100–30.

O'Connor, E. (2025) *Firecraft: Art, Body, and World Among Glassblowers*. New York: Columbia University Press.

Opazo, P. (2016) *Appetite for Innovation. Creativity & Change at ElBulli*. New York: Columbia University Press.

Ortner, S.B. (1984) "Theory in Anthropology since the Sixties," *Comparative Studies in Society and History*, 26(1), pp. 126–66.

Owen-Smith, J. and Powell, W.W. (2004) "Knowledge Networks as Channels and Conduits: The Effects of Spillovers in the Boston Biotechnology Community," *Organizational Science*, 15(1), pp. 5–21.

Park, R.E. and Burgess, E.W. (1925) *The City*. Chicago: University of Chicago Press.

Parker, J.N. and Hackett, E.J. (2012) "Hot Spots and Hot Moments in Scientific Collaborations and Social Movements," *American Sociological Review*, 77(1), pp. 21–44.

Pennycook, G., Fugelsang, J.A., and Koehler, D.J. (2015) "What Makes Us Think? A Three-Stage Dual-Process Model of Analytic Engagement," *Cognitive Psychology*, 80, pp. 34–72.

Perry-Smith, J.E. (2006) "Social yet Creative: The Role of Social Relationships in Facilitating Individual Creativity," *Academy of Management Journal*, 49(1), pp. 85–101.

Perry-Smith, J.E. and Shalley, C.E. (2003) "The Social Side of Creativity: A Static and Dynamic Social Network Perspective," *Academy of Management Review*, 28(1), pp. 89–106.

Peterson, R.A. (1990) "Why 1955? Explaining the Advent of Rock Music," *Popular Music*, 9(1), pp. 97–116.

Peterson, R.A. (1997) *Creating Country Music: Fabricating Authenticity*. Chicago: University of Chicago Press.

Peterson, R.A. and Anand, N. (2004) "The Production of Culture Perspective," *Annual Review of Sociology*, 30, pp. 311–34.

Peterson, R.A. and Berger, D.G. (1975) "Cycles in Symbol Production: The Case of Popular Music," *American Sociological Review*, 40(2), pp. 158–73.

Peterson, R.A. and Berger, D.G. (1996) "Measuring Industry Concentration,

Diversity, and Innovation in Popular Music," *American Sociological Review*, 61(1), pp. 175–8.

Petre, C. (2021) *All the News That's Fit to Click: How Metrics Are Transforming the Work of Journalists*. Princeton, NJ: Princeton University Press.

Phillips, D.J. (2013) *Shaping Jazz: Cities, Labels, and the Global Emergence of an Art Form*. Princeton, NJ: Princeton University Press.

Phillips, D.J. and Owens, D.A. (2004) "Incumbents, Innovation, and Competence: The Emergence of Recorded Jazz, 1920 to 1929," *Poetics*, 32(3–4), pp. 281–95.

Phillips, D.J. and Zuckerman, E. (2001) "Middle Status Conformity: Theoretical Restatement and Empirical Demonstration in Two Markets," *American Journal of Sociology*, 107(2), pp. 379–429.

Pinch, T.J. and Trocco, F. (2002) *Analog Days: The Invention and Impact of the Moog Synthesizer*. Cambridge, MA: Harvard University Press.

Policastro, E. (1999) "Intuition," in Runco, M.A. and Pritzker, S. (eds.) *The Encyclopaedia of Creativity*, vol. 2. San Diego, CA: Academic Press, pp. 89–93.

Powell, W.W., White, D.R., Koput, K.W., and Owen-Smith, J. (2005) "Network Dynamics and Field Evolution: The Growth of Interorganizational Collaboration in the Life Sciences," *American Journal of Sociology*, 110(4), pp. 1132–205.

Price, T. (2020) "Cognition in Situations," *Symbolic Interaction*, 43, pp. 692–720.

Pringle, A. and Sowden, P.T. (2017) "The Mode Shifting Index (MSI): A New Measure of the Creative Thinking Skill of Shifting between Associative and Analytic Thinking," *Thinking Skills and Creativity*, 23, pp. 17–28.

Rao, H., Monin, P., and Durand, R. (2005) "Border Crossing: Bricolage and the Erosion of Categorical Boundaries in French Gastronomy," *American Sociological Review*, 70(6), pp. 968–91.

Reckwitz, A. (2017) *The Invention of Creativity: Modern Society and the Culture of the New*. Cambridge: Polity Press.

Reynolds, S. (2011) *Retromania: Pop Culture's Addiction to its Own Past*. New York: Faber & Faber.

Rogers, E.M. (2003) *Diffusion of Innovations*, 5th edn. New York: Free Press.

Root-Bernstein, R. (2002) "Aesthetic Cognition," *International Studies in the Philosophy of Science*, 16(1), pp. 61–77.

Root-Bernstein, R. and Root-Bernstein, M. (1999) *Sparks of Genius: The Thirteen Thinking Tools of the World's Most Creative People*. Boston: Houghton Mifflin.

Rose-Greenland, F. (2013) "Seeing the Unseen: Prospective Loading and Knowledge Forms in Archaeological Discovery," *Qualitative Sociology*, 36, pp. 251–77.

Rose-Greenland, F. (2021) *Ruling Culture: Art Police, Tomb Robbers, and the Rise of Cultural Power in Italy*. Chicago: University of Chicago Press.

Ross, W. and Glăveanu, V. (2023) "The Constraints of Habit: Craft, Repetition,

and Creativity," *Phenomenology and the Cognitive Sciences*, 24, pp. 251–71.
Rossman, G. (2012) *Climbing the Charts: What Radio Airplay Tells Us about the Diffusion of Innovation*. Princeton, NJ: Princeton University Press.
Runco, M.A. (2006) "Reasoning and Personal Creativity," in Kaufman, J.C. and Baer, J. (eds.) *Creativity and Reason in Cognitive Development*. Cambridge: Cambridge University Press, pp. 99–116.
Runco, M.A. (2014) *Creativity: Theories and Themes: Research, Development, and Practice*. San Diego, CA: Elsevier Academic Press.
Santana-Acuña, Á. (2020) *Ascent to Glory: How One Hundred Years of Solitude Was Written and Became a Global Classic*. New York: Columbia University Press.
Sawyer, R.K. (2000) "Improvisation and the Creative Process: Dewey, Collingwood, and the Aesthetics of Spontaneity," *The Journal of Aesthetics and Art Criticism*, 58(2), pp. 149–61.
Sawyer, R.K. (2006) *Explaining Creativity: The Science of Human Innovation*. New York: Oxford University Press.
Sawyer, R.K. (2011) "The Cognitive Neuroscience of Creativity: A Critical Review," *Creativity Research Journal*, 23(2), pp. 137–54.
Sawyer, R.K. and DeZutter, S. (2009) "Distributed Creativity: How Collective Creations Emerge from Collaboration," *Psychology of Aesthetics, Creativity, and the Arts*, 3(2), pp. 81–92.
Scott, A.J. (2000) *The Cultural Economy of Cities: Essays on the Geography of Image-Producing Industries*. London; Thousand Oaks, CA: Sage.
Seabrook, J. (2012) "Factory Girls: Cultural Technology and the Making of Swedish Pop," *The New Yorker*, 26 March.
Seabrook, J. (2015) *The Song Machine: Inside the Hit Factory*. New York: W.W. Norton.
Seaver, N. (2018) "What Should an Anthropology of Algorithms Do?," *Cultural Anthropology*, 33(3), pp. 375–85.
Seaver, N. (2022) *Computing Taste: Algorithms and the Makers of Music Recommendation*. Chicago: University of Chicago Press.
Sennett, R. (2008) *The Craftsman*. New Haven, CT: Yale University Press.
Sewell, A. (2020) *Wendy Carlos: A Biography*. Oxford: Oxford University Press.
Sgourev, S.V. (2013a) "The Dynamics of Risk in Innovation: A Premiere or an Encore?," *Industrial and Corporate Change*, 22(2), pp. 549–75.
Sgourev, S.V. (2013b) "How Paris Gave Rise to Cubism (and Picasso): Ambiguity and Fragmentation in Radical Innovation," *Organization Science*, 24(6), pp. 1601–17.
Shapin, S. (1989) "The Invisible Technician," *American Scientist*, 77(6), pp. 554–63.
Shapin, S. (1994) *A Social History of Truth: Civility and Science in Seventeenth-Century England*. Chicago: University of Chicago Press.

Shapin, S. (2018) "Making Art/Discovering Science," *KNOW: A Journal on the Formation of Knowledge*, 2(2), pp. 177–205.
Shapin, S. (2020a) "The Rise and Rise of Creativity," *Aeon*, 12 October. Available at: https://aeon.co/essays/how-did-creativity-become-an-engine-of-economic-growth.
Shapin, S. (2020b) "Breakfast at Buck's: Informality, Intimacy, and Innovation in Silicon Valley," *Osiris*, 35, pp. 324–47.
Shapin, S. and Schaffer, S. (1985) *Leviathan and the Air-Pump: Hobbes, Boyle, and the Experimental Life*. Princeton, NJ: Princeton University Press.
Siciliano, M.L. (2016) "Disappearing into the Object: Aesthetic Subjectivities and Organizational Control in Routine Cultural Work," *Organization Studies*, 37(5), pp. 687–708.
Siciliano, M.L. (2021) *Creative Control: The Ambivalence of Work in Cultural Industries*. New York: Columbia University Press.
Silver, D. and Clark, T.N. (2016) *Scenescapes: How Qualities of Place Shape Social Life*. Chicago: University of Chicago Press.
Silver, D., Clark, T.N., and Graziul, C. (2011) "Scenes, Innovation, and Urban Development," in Andersson, D.E., Andersson, A.E., and Mellander, C. (eds.) *Handbook of Creative Cities*. Cheltenham, UK; Northampton, MA: Edward Elgar, pp. 229–58.
Simmel, G. (1904) "Fashion," *The International Quarterly*, 10(1), pp. 130–55.
Simmel, G. (1950) *The Sociology of Georg Simmel*, trans. and ed. K.H. Wolff. New York: Free Press.
Simonton, D.K. (1988) *Scientific Genius: A Psychology of Science*. Cambridge; New York: Cambridge University Press.
Sloman, S.A. (1996) "The Empirical Case for Two Systems of Reasoning," *Psychological Bulletin*, 119(1), pp. 3–22.
Smee, S. (2016) *The Art of Rivalry: Four Friendships, Betrayals, and Breakthroughs in Modern Art*. New York: Random House.
Sowden, P.T., Pringle, A., and Gabora, L. (2015) "The Shifting Sands of Creative Thinking: Connections to Dual-Process Theory," *Thinking and Reasoning*, 21(1), pp. 40–60.
Spencer, G.M. (2015) "Knowledge Neighbourhoods: Urban Form and Evolutionary Economic Geography," *Regional Studies*, 49(5), pp. 883–98.
Star, S.L. and Griesemer, J.R. (1989) "Institutional Ecology, 'Translations' and Boundary Objects," *Social Studies of Science*, 19(3), pp. 387–420.
Star, S.L. and Ruhleder, K. (1996) "Steps Toward an Ecology of Infrastructure," *Information Systems Research*, 7(1), pp. 111–34.
Star, S.L. and Strauss, A. (1999) "Layers of Silence, Arenas of Voice: The Ecology of Visible and Invisible Work," *Computer Supported Cooperative Work*, 8(1–2), pp. 9–30.

Sterne, J. (2012) *MP3: The Meaning of a Format*. Durham, NC: Duke University Press.

Summers-Effler, E. (2022) "The Morality of Birding: Aesthetic Engagement, Emotion, and Cognition," *Theory and Society*, 51, pp. 907–22.

Thagard, P. and Stewart, T.C. (2011) "The AHA! Experience: Creativity Through Emergent Binding in Neural Networks," *Cognitive Science*, 35, pp. 1–33.

Thompson, V.A. (2009) "Dual Process Theories: A Metacognitive Perspective," in Evans, J. and Frankish, K. (eds.) *In Two Minds: Dual Processes and Beyond*. Oxford: Oxford University Press, pp. 171–95.

Tik, M., Sladky, R., Luft, C.D.B., Willinger, D., Hoffmann, A., Banissy, M.J., Bhattacharya, J., and Windischberger, C. (2018) "Ultra-High-Field fMRI Insights on Insight: Neural Correlates of the Aha!-Moment," *Human Brain Mapping*, 39, pp. 3241–52.

Topolinski, S. and Reber, R. (2010) "Gaining Insight into the 'Aha' Experience," *Current Directions in Psychological Science*, 19(6), pp. 402–5.

Turner, F. (2006) *From Counterculture to Cyberculture: Stewart Brand, the Whole Earth Network, and the Rise of Digital Utopianism*. Chicago: University of Chicago Press.

Uzzi, B. and Spiro, J. (2005) "Collaboration and Creativity: The Small World Problem," *American Journal of Sociology*, 111(2), pp. 447–504.

Vaisey, S. (2009) "Motivation and Justification: A Dual-Process Model of Culture in Action," *American Journal of Sociology*, 114(6), pp. 1675–715.

Van der Shyff, D., Schiavo, A., Walton, A., Velardo, V., and Chemero, A. (2018) "Musical Creativity and the Embodied Mind: Exploring the Possibilities of 4E Cognition and Dynamical Systems Theory," *Music & Science*, 1, pp. 1–18.

Van Venrooij, A. and Schmutz, V. (2018) "Categorical Ambiguity in Cultural Fields: The Effects of Genre Fuzziness in Popular Music," *Poetics*, 66, pp. 1–18.

Wacquant, L. (2004) *Body and Soul: Ethnographic Notebooks of an Apprentice-Boxer*. Oxford: Oxford University Press.

White, H.C. and White, C.A. (1965) *Canvases and Careers: Institutional Change in the French Painting World*. Chicago: University of Chicago Press.

Wohl, H. (2021) *Bound by Creativity: How Contemporary Art is Created and Judged*. Chicago: University of Chicago Press.

Wood, W. and Rünger, D. (2016) "Psychology of Habit," *Annual Review of Psychology*, 67, pp. 289–314.

Zuckerman, E.W. (1999) "The Categorical Imperative: Securities Analysts and the Illegitimacy Discount," *American Journal of Sociology*, 104(5), pp. 1398–438.

Zuckerman, E. (2016) "Optimal Distinctiveness Revisited: An Integrative Framework for Understanding the Balance between Differentiation and Conformity in Individual and Organizational Identities," in Pratt, M.G.,

Schultz, M., Ashforth, B.E., and Ravasi, D. (eds.) *The Oxford Handbook of Organizational Identity*. Oxford: Oxford University Press, pp. 183–99.
Zuckerman, E.W., Kim, T.-Y., Ukanwa, K., and von Rittmann, J. (2003) "Robust Identities or Nonentities? Typecasting in the Feature-Film Labor Market," *American Journal of Sociology*, 108(5), pp. 1018–73.

Index

Index